Bear Grease, Builders and Bandits

The Men and Women of Wichita's Past

By Beccy Tanner

ISBN 1-880652-09-9
Library of Congress Catalog No. 91-66990

Printed in the United States of America by Mennonite Press, Inc., Newton, Kansas

Cover and sectional art by Jeff Pulaski
Book design by John Hiebert
Edited by Arlice Davenport and Chuck Potter

Acknowledgements

Many people have contributed to this book, especially Bill Ellington, historian at the Wichita Public Library, whom we quote extensively.

Special thanks go to Ellington; Joe Snell, past executive director of the Kansas State Historical Society; Paul Oberg, supervisor of museum programs for the Wichita public schools; the late Waldo Koop, Wichita historian; Susan Shaw, Wichita Eagle reporter; Deb Bagby and Brenda White, Wichita Eagle library assistants; Laura Addison, Eagle reporter; Mark Gale, Eagle staff photographer; James P. Girard, the Eagle's systems editor; and Beverly Henline and Wilma Sehnert, history researchers.

We also thank the Kansas State Historical Society, Old Cowtown Museum and the Wichita-Sedgwick County Historical Museum.

The photographs on Pages 10, 11, 12, 13, 15 (downtown Wichita), 18 (Munger house), 46, 53, 54, 55, 56 (Carey Hotel), 88 (Charles Payne, Payne's Paradise), 123 (J.R. Mead house), 138 (Bitting Building), 149 and 150 are used by permission of the Wichita-Sedgwick County Historical Museum; the photographs on Pages 15 (Marshall Murdock), 42 (Bat Masterson), 45 (Wyatt Earp), 65 ("Pap" Singleton), 112, 114 and 127 (President Woodrow Wilson) are courtesy of the Kansas State Historical Society; the photographs on Page 17 are from the book "Searching for Home" by Martha Nelson Vogt and Christina Vogt; the illustration on Page 25 is courtesy of Mark Alley; the illustration of Kellogg Traditional Magnet School on Page 30 is courtesy of the Wichita public schools; the illustrations on Pages 47 ("Rowdy Joe" Lowe) and 85 (Silas Bliss) are courtesy of Bill Ellington; the photograph of the Roe Institute on Page 63 is courtesy of Valerie Bilyew; the photograph of Charlie Patton's tailor shop on Page 65 is courtesy of George Johnson of Valley Center; all other photographs and illustrations are courtesy of the Wichita Public Library or are from The Wichita Eagle. Although The Eagle has been known by slightly different names in its history, for simplicity's sake we have referred to it throughout as The Wichita Eagle.

Introduction

Sometimes the people and places of the past can strike us as bigger than life. We hear the stories and we learn the facts—but often there is a wall between us and our history.

For instance, we may know that Jesse Chisholm settled the area, established Wichita's first trading post and had a local creek and trail named after him. But it's not until we hear that he died from eating rancid bear grease that we begin to realize just what kind of life he and other early Wichitans must have led.

It's hard for us to imagine what bear grease—let alone rancid bear grease—must have tasted like. But for early settlers, bear meat cooked in its own grease was a rare treat in an otherwise bland prairie diet.

That's one example of how the facts of history don't always translate into real people—people who battled grasshopper plagues, droughts and floods, who fought against blizzards and a depressed economy.

But somehow they survived—much as we do today. They paid bills, gave birth to babies, tinkered with inventions and wondered how downtown Wichita would ever get going.

Some say Wichita was a town built on hot air.

Perhaps it was.

It didn't have any mountains to attract those searching for gold and silver. And there was no ocean beckoning with sandy beaches.

But the area did have wide-open spaces, a fertile river valley and lots of promise. From that promise sprang a wide assortment of characters who gathered, lived and died on the confluence of two rivers.

Their legacy is the subject of this book. Most of the events in these stories took place between 1865 and 1930. Some occurred later than that, but on the whole, we have tried to look at the time before the aviation industry came to Wichita.

It was an era of rich and diverse developments, from the incorporation of the town in 1870 to the work projects in the Great Depression.

We look at a current-day grocery store parking lot and try to imagine what the area must have been like in 1868, when the site was known as Camp Beecher—an outpost for drunken and bored soldiers.

We grin at stories about outlaws such as Jack Ledford, who wooed the prettiest girl in town by literally sweeping her off her feet at a full gallop to ride across Wichita's dust-covered streets. And, of course, we marvel at the gallery of bandits and scoundrels, including Rowdy Joe Lowe, who earned his nickname by biting the nose off a man he brawled with.

But Wichita has also sprouted its share of passionate causes. Mary Elizabeth Lease, for one, helped start one of the first women's organizations in the state, the Hypatia Club. Lease later became a national figure in the Populist movement.

Wichitans are already familiar with the antics of prohibitionist Carry A. Nation. In addition to her story, we look at one of her friends, Myra McHenry, a somewhat lesser-known figure who often caused Wichita city fathers a great deal of anxiety.

Wichita sprang up from a variety of cultures and races. American Indians played an important role in the city's growth—from the days of peace treaties with the Kiowa chief Satanta to the building and promoting of the American Indian Institute in north Wichita. And for decades, Wichita's black business district thrived and prospered before falling to the designs of urban renewal.

Wichita has had its share of eccentrics, from Cannonball Green, the city's first stagecoach man; to "Durable" Del Crozier, a politician who never won an election; to Father Bliss, who amazed residents of the day with his junk collection. And it also had its share of unique and ornate buildings, designed and used by people with colorful tales.

Indeed, Wichita builders made a lasting mark on the area. We examine the city's oldest building, the Occidental Hotel, and note the people who once slept there. We sympathize with a boy who writes his mother a letter telling her why he doesn't want to live in the Wichita Children's Home anymore. And we measure the length and width of the Michigan Building—the city's skinniest skyscraper.

It's that type of rich heritage, mixed with a dose of Yankee ingenuity, that helped Wichitans survive the Kansas elements, live through schemes and scandals and create lasting works of arts.

When we read their stories, we discover that Wichita was built on, and thrived because of, the strength of its people.

They were real people who cared enough to stay. They were people who pursued their dreams. They were people like you and me, not all that much bigger than life.

Table of Contents

The Cow Town, Judge Riggs and Orphan Trains

Portrait of a cow town 10
The naming of Wichita 12
The town's incorporation and
   Judge Reuben Riggs 13
The 1889 bust 14
The orphan trains 16
WPA projects 18

Buffalo Herds, Grasshopper Plagues and Drunken Soldiers

Jesse Chisholm, trader 22
Elias Hicks Durfee, trader 23
Andrew Greenway, trader 24
Camp Beecher 25
Edmund Mosley, settler 26
Eli Waterman, settler 27
William Finn, schoolteacher 28
Fred Augustus Sowers, newspaper editor . . . 28
The Wichita Beacon 29
Milo Kellogg, postmaster 30
D.S. Munger, settler 31
Andrew Fabrique, pioneer doctor 32
The Allen brothers, mayors 33
Park City 34
Cattle drives 35
Doc Lewellen, trader and sheriff 36
Grasshopper invasion 37

Gunslingers, Saloon Keeps and Thieves

Judge "Tiger Bill" Campbell 40
Henry Clay Sluss, lawyer 40
William Hays, sheriff and mill operator 41
Bat Masterson, lawman 42
Jack Ledford, outlaw 43
Mike and John Meagher, lawmen 44

Wyatt Earp, lawman 45
Catherine McCarty and Billy the Kid 46
Rowdy Joe Lowe, outlaw 47

Prostitutes, Prohibitionists and Populists

Rea Woodman, author 50
Mary Elizabeth Lease, Hypatia Club founder 50
Jessie Clark, music teacher 52
Myra Warren McHenry, crusader 52
Lucetta Fassett Carter, magazine salesman . . . 53
Inez "Dixie Lee" Oppenheimer, prostitute . . 54
Carry A. Nation, prohibitionist 55
Hattie Waller, mystery girl 57

Chief Satanta, Indian Tunes and a Bowl of Chili

Satanta 60
The Wichita Indians 61
Henry Roe Cloud, educator 62
Thurlow Lieurance, musician and composer 63
William Dye and his chili factory 64
Wichita's black business district 65

Hotels, Cathedrals and Skyscrapers

Occidental Hotel 68
Carey-Eaton Hotel 68
Wichita Children's Home 70
Central Building 71
Allis Hotel 72
St. Mary's Cathedral 73
Keen Kutter Building 75
Live Stock Exchange Building 76
Caldwell-Murdock Building 77
Michigan Building 78
All Hallows Academy 78
Lewis Academy 79
Kansas Sanitarium 81

Eccentrics, Sea Captains and Recluses

Cannonball Green, stagecoach owner 84
Father Bliss, dentist. 84
Edwin Rutherford Powell, sea captain 85
Dan Cupp, settler 86
George Litzenberg, newspaperman 87
Charles Payne, animal collector 88
J. Hudson and Eva McKnight, wealthy
    recluses 89
Bliss Isley, newspaperman 90
Ed Shutz and his memorial. 91
Earl Browder, communist. 93
"Durable" Del Crozier, politician. 94

Beaches, Bricks and Flicks

Turner Opera House 96
Sandy Beach 97
Dockum drugstores. 97
Arkansas Valley Interurban 98
Ackerman Island 100
The Forum 101
John Mack Bridge .102
Train depots 103
Miller Theater 104
Orpheum Theater .106

Hot Air, Schemes and Scandals

William Greiffenstein, father of Wichita 110
Marshall Murdock, newspaper editor. 111
Garfield University .112
David Payne, adventurer. 114
Wichita Watch Factory 114
Scott Winne, one-time golden boy 116
Lorenzo Lewelling, Kansas governor 117
Rajah Rabbitry. 118

Soldiers, Scouts and Developers

Kit Carson, Indian scout. 122
J.R. Mead, pioneer 123
William Mathewson, plainsman and scout. . .124
The Grand Army of the Republic 125
Col. E.E. and Erwin Bleckley, businessman
    and war hero 126
President Woodrow Wilson 127
A.A. Hyde, inventor of Mentholatum. 128

Governors, Lawyers and Cooks

Patrick Valentine Healy, real estate dealer . . .130
Nathaniel English, Wichita developer 130
Robert Lawrence, west side developer 132
Thomas Fitch, investment broker 133
Benajah Aldrich, railroad tycoon and
    mayor. 134
James Oakley Davidson, banker and
    investor 135
Ola Martinson, land speculator 136
Henry Allen, newspaperman 137
The Bitting brothers, downtown merchants 137
Orsemus Hills Bentley, historian. 139
William Stanley, Kansas governor. 139
F.W. "Woody" Hockaday, mapmaker 140
Col. Sam Amidon, businessman. 141
J.J. Jones, automaker. 142
White Castle hamburgers 144

Artists, Actors and Opera Stars

John Noble, painter 148
Sidney Toler, actor .148
C.A. Seward, painter. 149
Kathleen Kersting, opera singer 151

The Cow Town, Judge Riggs and Orphan Trains

"Purists have been pointing out recently that the Indians pronounced Wichita as though it were spelled Wi-she-tah. Others would have it Wishita. Then there is Weeshita, and also Weechita and Wicheeta. Foreigners sometimes would have it Veechita or a sound resembling a sudden sneeze. But after you try them all on your saxophone, you find that the perfectly natural way of pronouncing it is the old familiar Witch-itaw."
—*The Wichita Beacon*
Oct. 25, 1926

Portrait of a Cow Town

Fledgling city was in the right place at the right time

Andrew Greenway, a trader who operated a ferry across the Arkansas River from 1868 to 1872, was one of the first to describe the city of Wichita.

On Aug. 28, 1868, he wrote a letter to the Junction City Weekly Union about the small town: "I see that you never say anything about our city. Probably you do not know where it is, as it is a new place, at the mouth of the Little Arkansas, where five years ago the country was covered with buffalo, is now looming into importance."

In 1868, "importance" meant 30 residents. By 1870, that number had swelled to 689.

People came to Wichita from everywhere—from Germany, Wisconsin, Virginia, Kentucky, Ohio and Ireland. Some came from England, Switzerland and Belgium. And a few came from Indian Territory, what is now Oklahoma.

The small town on the river happened to be in the right place at the right time.

It began just after the Civil War, when people were looking for a fresh start. Kansas was a new state then, and those who came to Wichita were hoping to start over in a place with new opportunities.

Indeed, Wichita was a community with promise.

In 1870, more people in the new community—110 to be precise—practiced farming than any other occupation. There were 63 farm laborers, 101 housekeepers, one wagon maker and five teamsters.

The town attracted two photographers, one dentist, three butchers, two stonemasons and seven attorneys.

Records from the 1870 census show the town also had two blacksmiths, three saddle- and harnessmakers, 11 cattle dealers, one stage driver, and six dry goods and grocery dealers. Wichita also had four domestic servants, three physicians, 33 carpenters, two schoolteachers, one house painter, one justice of the peace, five real estate agents, three clerks, one minister and three saloon keepers.

But the census also reveals other, less celebratory glimpses into the lives of early Wichitans. For instance, 368 could not read or write. That number included heads of households and their children.

And housing was scarce. Most of those coming to the new town

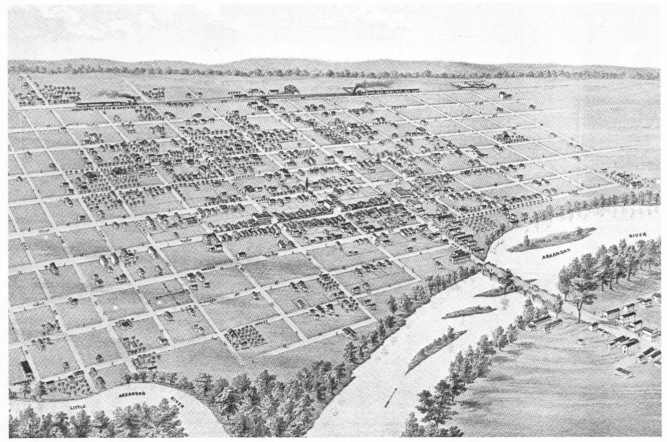

An 1873 map of Wichita by E.S. Glover showed the growth of the town along the river.

were between the ages of 20 and 40. For them, the term "family" most often meant that two to three generations lived under one roof Sometimes it even meant two or more families of different names living under one roof.

That was the case with the John McCormick and George Mitts families. Both men were 28 years old in 1870. John was married to Mary, and they had one child, Elfie. George was married to Hettie, and they had one child, William.

Both families came from Iowa. There was no value placed on their home; the McCormicks' personal property, however, was valued at $300.

The Mahoney family came from Ireland. There was Timothy, 31, a farmer; Batholomew Jr., 24, a stonemason; Batholomew, 65, a farm laborer; Michael, 22, a stonemason; and Catharine, 50, a housekeeper. Like so many of that time, the Mahoneys pooled their talents and resources to make a fresh start.

Their home was valued at $200. In 1870, the family's personal property value was $2,000.

The McCormick, Mahoney and Mitts families, all of them white, were typical residents of that time. Almost all of Wichita in 1870 was white, with the exception of three American Indians and five blacks. One of those Indians was Catherine

Cowboys water cattle in Chisholm Creek. Wichita was along the Chisholm Trail from Texas to Abilene, so cattle drives through town were frequent.

Greiffenstein, also one of the wealthiest residents. Her personal property was valued at $6,000. Her husband, William, the town's co-founder, was a dealer in groceries. He had $20,000 in real estate and $10,000 in personal property.

The only black family in town was the Richard Robinsons. They lived in the same house as James Gordy, John Cox, Daniel Boatwright and Jermiah Kunkel, all white men from Indiana and Pennsylvania.

Whatever their color, all residents of the new town believed it needed to be official to keep growing. That's why on July 21, 1870, one woman, Catherine McCarty—mother of future outlaw Billy the Kid—and 123 men signed a petition to create a town and presented it to Judge Reuben Riggs. The judge then issued the town's articles of incorporation.

After that, the town continued to grow, and Wichitans did what they had to to survive.

That meant living most often in dugouts or simple log cabins. And local history accounts say early Wichitans were often plagued by bluebottle flies that flocked around the hundreds of fresh buffalo hides laid out along Wichita streets. There is little record of what the town smelled like then, but it is supposed the smell wasn't good—especially in hot summer months.

Early residents also had to con-

tend with huge cattle drives that wound their way along the Chisholm Trail from Texas to Abilene.

Another indication of early-day life in Wichita is the medical accounts of residents as they battled with the elements and disease. Judge Riggs, the man who issued the town's articles of incorporation, died in a blizzard in 1872. He froze to death on the prairie, while his son, Isaac, lost both of his feet to frostbite.

In 1870, Nancy Ann Rogers came to Wichita. She was a nurse for the W.C. Woodman family. A few years after she arrived in town, she noticed a pain in her left breast. Rogers went to one of the town doctors, who diagnosed her as having cancer. He told her he would charge her $25 to cut the cancer out. It was money the woman just didn't have.

Rea Woodman, a noted author, historian and journalist for The Wichita Eagle, later wrote about Rogers.

Woodman said that after Rogers "left Dr. Owen's place she hired a furnished room in the first block on north Main Street, at a dollar and a half a week." The woman paid a week's rent in advance and told the proprietor that she would be back the next day. She drove home and cooked enough food to last her two boys, William and Samuel, a week or more.

Catherine McCarty and 123 men signed a petition to create the town.

In the late 1870s, wagons filled Douglas Avenue at Wichita Street, now the John F. Kennedy Plaza at Century II.

she had let.

"She unpacked the butcher knife, and the white rags, and arranged the scant furniture to suit her purpose. Then she arranged the bedding, partially undressed, sat down on the edge of the bed and cut off the cancerous breast.

"Nearly a year afterward she told mother about it," Woodman wrote. "A few months before her death, mother told me about it."

Hard times aside, the town continued to grow. Of course, in later years, there were droughts, floods and grasshoppers. But through it all, the people stayed.

One of the town's developers, James R. Mead, said in a speech in 1884: "Cities are not the result of chance nor do they make themselves. Their prosperity and greatness are in a large measure due to the sagacity and enterprise of their founders and early settlers in reaching out and drawing to them the channels of commerce and trade."

Out of those early beginnings, hard work paid off. The city today boasts 300,000 residents. Not bad, from a humble start of 30.

The next morning she packed some food and clothing in a tin bucket, and a butcher knife and some white rags in a basket, and had William drive her to town. She told him that she was going to visit Woodman for a week, and that she had some trading to do, so he should let her off at the corner of Main and Douglas.

It was a lie, Woodman later wrote, but Rogers did not want to alarm her son.

Rogers then went to the room

The Naming of Wichita

Meaning is an enigma, but it came from an Indian tribe

In the mid-1860s, names were tossed back and forth as early occupants debated what to call the small village sprouting along the banks of the Arkansas River.

John Barnum, a Civil War veteran, plainsman and scout who was living in the area at the time, suggested "Opi Ela."

"What I really had in mind was naming the town for the handsomest squaw I ever saw," Barnum admitted in a Wichita Eagle article on June 13, 1926. "She was the daughter of the Wichita chief, and her name was Opi Ela, which means Elk's Tooth, but the name was too much for us.

"So, the early leaders named the town after her tribe, the Wichitas."

OK, so far.

But Wichitans have since had difficulty deciding what the name means.

What people have agreed on is that the name comes from the Wichita Indian tribe camped along the banks of the Arkansas River during the mid-1860s between what is now Murdock and 13th Street.

In 1910, Orsemus Hills Bentley, author of "History of Wichita and Sedgwick County," wrote that one Wichitan had consulted the Bureau of American Ethnology and said that the Indian word "Wichita" meant "tattooed faces."

Bentley wrote: " 'Tattooed faces' comes from a Kiowa word which was applied to the Wichita, Waco, Tawakoni and Kichai Indians on account of their habit of tattooing

their faces and mouths."

That definition incensed developer J.R. Mead, who said Wichita meant "scattered lodges."

On July 6, 1924, The Wichita Beacon ran an article by Bliss Isely, noted Wichita author, historian and newspaperman, who said, "Wichita means paint face. Some authorities have said it means scattered lodges. Others have said it means bear eyes. Some even that it means other people."

The meaning still was not resolved two years later. On Feb. 14, 1926, Henry Roe Cloud wrote an article for The Eagle explaining more of the history of the name. Roe was one of the nation's leading American Indians of that time. He founded the Roe Institute, later known as the American Indian In-

J.R. Mead made the final decision to name Wichita.

The city name Wichita first appeared in print in 1868 on an advertising circular distributed to cattlemen.

stitute, at 3500 E. 21st.

Roe wrote that "The Osage Indians with whom the Otoes, Poncas, Omahas, the Sioux and Winnebagos were affiliated, called the reeds of the lake regions 'wee chee chee.' " He said that those who dwelt in reed wigwams were called "wee-chiyo-chee," or "dwellers in reed wigwams."

Today, local historians say that regardless of the confusion about the meaning of Wichita, the final decision to name the town was made by Mead. The name first appeared in print in 1868 on an advertising circular distributed to cattlemen moving their herds to Northern markets.

Origins aside, the name also posed a pronunciation problem. On Oct. 25, 1926, The Wichita Beacon reported:

"Purists have been pointing out recently that the Indians pronounced Wichita as though it were spelled Wi-she-tah. Others would have it Wishita. Then there is Weeshita, and also Weechita and Wicheeta. Foreigners sometimes would have it Veechita or a sound resembling a sudden sneeze. But after you try them all on your saxophone, you find that the perfectly natural way of pronouncing it is the old familiar Witch-itaw."

Judge Reuben Riggs

He lived and died as a genuine pioneer

The word "pioneer" is etched on Reuben Riggs' gravestone.

It was the pioneer spirit that led Riggs to become the Wichita area's first lawyer and judge during the late 1860s and early 1870s. And it was the pioneer spirit that led to his death.

Originally from Iowa, Riggs, his wife, Nancy, and a son, Mahlon, headed west during the Pikes Peak gold rush of the early 1860s. In 1864, the family left Colorado and settled in Marion County. Riggs, 54, was the only attorney in the area.

Four years later, Nancy died and Riggs moved to Sedgwick County, where he opened the county's first law and land office.

In April 1870, when an election was called for county officers and for a permanent county seat, Riggs was elected judge, and Wichita won out over Park City.

On July 21, 1870, Catherine McCarty and 123 men signed a petition to create a town and presented it to Riggs, who issued the town's articles of incorporation.

The movers and shakers behind the petition included Uncle Jack Peyton, Col. Morgan Cox, Edward

Smith, Charles A. Stafford and Christopher Pierce.

At the time, 607 people lived in Sedgwick County, with the population growing daily. There was a sprinkling of homes, and the living conditions were primitive.

"It was almost a necessity then that some type of town be started to provide some guidance for the settlers and to help solve any problems that might transpire," said Bill Ellington, historian at the Wichita Public Library.

Of the leading players:

Stafford was an attorney and real-estate dealer. He wrote the petition for the town's incorporation. Stafford and his brother, William, a farmer, came to Wichita from Fountain County, Ind., in June 1870.

Smith had a grocery and general outfitting store in a frame building on Main Street. Little else is known about him.

Cox was owner of the Douglas Avenue Hotel and supervised the construction of the Occidental Hotel at 306 N. Main—the city's first three-story building and first brick building. Cox came to Wichita from Indiana in July 1870. He was active in local commercial and political affairs and instrumental in establishing the Masons in Wichita.

Peyton was a saddle maker and known for his gift of gab and ability to swear. Like Smith, little is known about Peyton except that he walked with a limp.

Pierce arrived in Wichita in 1869. He worked for his brother-in-law, William Greiffenstein, and operated a store at the north end of town.

Reuben Riggs froze to death when he and other businessmen were overtaken by a blizzard in 1872.

They made up the small town's embryo government and were trustees until a year later when the town was upgraded to a city.

The 1870 order of incorporation read simply:

"Be it remembered, that at a special term of the probate court, held in the town of Wichita on the 21st day of July, A.D. 1870, a petition was presented to the court by the inhabitants of the town of Wichita describing the said town by mete and boundaries and praying that they may be incorporated and a police established. . . ."

Riggs issued the incorporation, and the first meeting of the board of trustees of Wichita was held the following day at McAdams Hall on Main Street.

Although the community was officially recognized as a town, the old record book with the minutes is titled "First Record City of Wichita."

Stafford was the presiding chairman.

On April 3, 1871, the town became a third-class city with Dr. E.B. Allen serving as mayor. The first councilmen were W.B. Hutchison, S.C. Johnson, Charles Schattner, Andrew Fabrique, George Shlichter and George Vantillburgh.

This was the beginnings of a town, in turn the beginnings of a city.

Riggs' time as a judge in Wichita was short-lived, however. In January 1872, he and a son, Isaac, went with a group of other business opportunists to Medicine Lodge Creek in Barber County to help lay out a town. En route, the party was overtaken by a blizzard, and Riggs froze to death.

The Wichita Eagle reported on Jan. 9, 1872: "Judge Riggs and his party were overtaken by the late cold snap before they reached their destination.

"Several of the party were badly frozen, but more especially the Judge, whose limbs were so frosted that he could not be taken back to his home until the weather had softened. Judge Riggs is an old resident of the state. He was respected by all who knew him as a man of sterling worth."

The newspaper also reported that Isaac Riggs had both of his feet amputated.

The Bust of 1889

Wichita hit bottom during one bitter summer

In recent years, Wichita has suffered boom and bust, but Wichitans in 1889 had it worse. Much worse.

The city was in the midst of a drought that was to last four years. Temperatures were soaring, crops were failing, and the bottom had fallen out of the land market.

"They were hurting bad," said the late Curtise Wood, author of "Dynamics of Faith," an economic study of Wichita from 1870 to 1897. "The people who had built the city were either broke, old or had moved away. A new generation was left to carry on. And they were the ones to feel all the bitterness or loss. They set the tone for Wichita for the next 20 years."

Although Wichitans recently have had to face a drought and an unpredictable economy of their own, local historians say the problems now pale in comparison to the ones in 1889. The psychological impact of the summer of 1889, they say, is still felt.

Before then, Wichita, like much of the rest of the Midwest, had been enjoying a boom period. European crop failures had boosted U.S. food exports, which encouraged people to settle lands previously occupied by Indians, Wood said.

From 1881 to 1887, 203,000 people settled in Kansas. In 1889, Wichita's population was estimated by the Sedgwick County tax assessor to be 48,000.

"Back East there was a surplus of money," Wood said. "Eastern people were hunting for a place to invest."

Wichita was one of them.

In June 1887, Wichita ranked third in the nation in volume of real estate transactions. New York City was first, Kansas City second. Chicago, Philadelphia and Brooklyn, N.Y., rounded out the top six. In one year—from June 1886 to June 1887—1,871 residences, 100 businesses, 22 factories and 11 hotels were constructed in Wichita.

"Wichita was typical of many of the Western towns," Wood said. "There was a booster spirit where everything was possible."

Six railroads linked the city to the rest of the nation; six colleges and

Downtown Wichita of the late 1800s was a booming place, and a variety of transportation was available to visitors.

Marshall Murdock, Wichita Eagle editor, at first praised the "pluck and energy" of Wichita developers.

universities were built, and two more were proposed; the City Council was actively pursuing land to add to the city limits and on Feb. 21, 1887, annexed 288 additions. And plans for new businesses such as a watch factory, brick works, a vinegar factory and railroad car company held the promise of growing employment.

The growth came with the blessings of the city leaders. On Oct. 9, 1887, Marshall Murdock, the editor of The Wichita Eagle, wrote of the

city's rise to fame and fortune in an editorial:

"Pluck and energy, it is said, build cities. . . . It has been and is now the plucky and energetic men who saw advantages of her (Wichita's) location, situation, and environments who are reaping the rich rewards."

But in the flurry of activity, Wood said, "There were promises made that had no relationship to reality. There was a virus working where people lost all semblance of balance.''

By the winter of 1887, Murdock was beginning to feel uneasy with the boom and urged residents in an editorial to ''call a halt.''

''When men abandon legitimate trade to embark in a craze of any character the end is not far off,'' he wrote. ''No work, however well directed, no brain, however powerful or far seeing, can avert the collapse which must follow an overstrained inflation.''

Nevertheless, it would be some time before land speculation and Eastern investments would grind to a halt in Wichita.

Some of the effects were felt in 1888, but the total impact wasn't felt until 1889. That year, businesses and schools began to fall by the wayside.

There was a panic. Many of Wichita's capitalists were losing thousands of dollars. Some, in frustration, pulled up stakes and sold

their homes. And many homes that had just been constructed were unoccupied.

By then, the drought and crop failure had spread to other parts of Kansas. Families were leaving their farms and coming to Wichita in hope of going back East or of moving into Oklahoma's Indian Territory.

''The western Kansas farmers were going broke and were riding into town with skinny kids,'' Wood said. ''They wanted the lands that belonged to the Indians to be opened up and were putting all sorts of pressure on officials to do so.''

To ease tensions, Wood said, the Oklahoma Territory was opened in 1889 and the Cherokee Strip in 1893.

By 1892, thousands of people had left the city, and the population was listed at 20,928.

Wichita lost a lot of good people

that year, including William Greiffenstein, the city's co-founder.

To some extent, Wood said, Wichita is still feeling the effects of the bust of 1889.

''My notion is that Wichita never fully recovered, particularly psychologically,'' he said. Through the years, the city has traditionally remained conservative.

''You do not have the expansive feeling that it once was,'' Wood said. ''There isn't the room to expand horizons. The horizons have been pulled back. I don't think we will ever recapture that spirit again.''

Could the economic collapse happen again?

''I think it could,'' Ellington said. ''But not in comparison to that original bust. We have buffered ourselves real well. We learned some lessons from it. It was an experience that made us cautious, which is still affecting our growth today.''

Orphan Trains

Railways carried children to a better way of life

For children in crowded East Coast orphanages, small towns in Kansas offered a better life.

That philosophy led to the ''orphan trains'' that brought between 6,000 and 7,000 orphans to Kansas between 1854 and 1929.

They were among nearly 100,000 orphans placed on passenger trains headed to the Midwest during that period. The children were promised educational and religious opportunities on farms and in small towns.

The orphan trains didn't stop in Kansas City, Wichita and the other big cities. Instead, they took the children to farming communities such as Belle Plaine, Newton, Sterling, Concordia and McPherson.

The trains were the brainchild of the Rev. Charles Loring Brace, founder of the Children's Aid Society in New York. At his suggestion, the placement in foster homes was

free—so more children could be adopted.

Brace believed the children should be sent to rural homes,

where there was always room for one more pair of hands to help with the chores.

Native Kansan Martha Nelson

Mary Turner Ratley was 4 when she was sent to Fredonia, where Clarence and Ora Bounds adopted her. A longtime Wichitan, she died in 1989.

Ida and Bill Bishop had a pet calf on their farm near Sterling. She later was a school librarian in Wichita; he moved to Phoenix and became a meat inspector.

Ida Elder and her brother, Bill, were adopted by Ward and Flossie Bishop, a Sterling farm couple. Ida Bishop Walton later moved to Wichita and became a school librarian. Her brother moved to Phoenix and was a meat inspector. Both have since died.

Vogt said the orphans, 15 or 20 in a group, traveled on trains that also carried regular passengers. The ones bound for Kansas were often chaperoned by Anna Hill, a Children's Aid Society member from New York who corresponded with the children, visited them in their adopted homes and even bought some of the girls their wedding dresses.

Some critics said that children from the orphan trains were treated poorly, placed in unsuitable homes and given little or no supervision afterwards. Farmers, they said, might treat teenage orphans as virtual slave laborers.

Vogt of Hillsboro is co-author of "Searching for Home" with her daughter, Christina. She says that at each railway station and sometimes in churches, schools or opera houses, the children were lined up to be chosen by families. Those not chosen were loaded back on the train to repeat the procedure at the next stop.

"In many of these small towns, the arrival of these trains was a big social event," Vogt said. "People were excited. It was an honor to take in these children."

Even so, this segment of American history was not often talked about, nor was it recorded at length, she said.

"There was a stigma then that adoption was not OK," Vogt said. "People did not want to say they had come out here on the orphan trains. When I started researching this in 1973, I had people hang up the phone on me. They just couldn't face it. . . . But yet, not one of the people I talked with said they preferred the orphanage to the chance they took in coming out here."

Although Wichita wasn't included in Brace's plan, some of the orphans found their way into the area.

One, Mary Turner Ratley, was 4 years old when she was sent to Fre-donia in 1916. Ratley, a longtime resident of Wichita who died in 1989, recalled those experiences in an article in The Wichita Eagle on Dec. 22, 1979.

Ratley's foster parents, Clarence and Ora Bounds, had been married 11 years in 1916 and were childless. She described the first time she and the Boundses saw each other:

"They said they walked up on the porch and the screen door came flying open. I flew out and ran right between my Daddy's legs."

Anna Fuchs, who lives in Lindsborg, was 11 in 1924 when she made the trip from New York City to McPherson.

"Everybody wanted to get out of the orphanage," Fuchs said. "We had food and clothing, but after you've lost your parents . . . I realized that if I didn't get out, I wouldn't have much of a chance in life. I was eager to get some education."

She was adopted by Jennie Bengtson, a 49-year-old spinster who supported herself by taking in boarders. Fuchs graduated from McPherson College in 1937 in music and education. As years went by and Bengtson began to go blind, Fuchs took care of her. Bengtson died on Dec. 10, 1964.

For more than a quarter century, until the orphans no longer were sent West, Anna Laura Hill served as an escort for the children.

In a letter to the New York Tribune in 1883, Brace, the society's founder, said: "We would be the first to hear of such cases, and such are scarcely ever reported to us."

Nevertheless, by the 1920s the orphan trains were becoming fewer and fewer—partly because of child labor laws and a growing movement to keep families together.

When the train program started, it was hoped that the movement would improve the children's lives, Vogt said. "Brace wanted to bring children to a farm area where they would have enough food, learn how to work and become a useful part of the community. As orphans they weren't getting those things.

"Not a one of them said to me, 'I wish they hadn't brought me.' "

Her voice grows adamant when she talks about the orphan trains and their success. In fact, she contends, with so many children left homeless in today's society, the trains might be a good solution again.

"Work teaches a child self-respect," Vogt said. "And these children who were working on farms and living in small communities were learning to respect their own abilities. With so much going on today, I wish they'd bring the trains back."

WPA Projects

The New Deal was just that for Kansas

In the 1930s, Edgar Langsdorf held a master's degree in history from the University of Kansas, but no job.

He was not alone.

It was the Depression.

Kansas, like much of the rest of the Plains, had been hit by huge, unrelenting clouds of black dust that affected not only crops but morale. And the statewide unemployment rate reached 26 percent in 1932.

It was in that year that President Franklin D. Roosevelt announced his New Deal and its many alphabet agencies. The idea was to bring work and people together. The agencies included:

The Agricultural Adjustment Act (AAA), the National Recovery Act (NRA), the Reconstruction Finance Corporation (RFC), the Public Works Administration (PWA), the Works Progress Administration (WPA), the Home Owners Loan Corporation (HOLC), the National Youth Administration (NYA) and the Civilian Conservation Corps (CCC).

All had an impact on Kansas and Wichita, including Langsdorf, who went to work for the WPA. "It boosted morale," he said.

Dan Fitzgerald, local records archivist for the Kansas State Historical Society, said Roosevelt's New Deal changed Kansas and Wichita's look. It even changed people's perceptions of themselves.

"It helped us get out of an agricultural slump that affected most of Kansas," Fitzgerald said. "It em-

At the peak of the Depression the WPA employed many Wichita men to haul dirt to obliterate Ackerman Island.

The New Deal can be credited with the construction of Morrison Hall at Wichita State University.

ployed thousands of people who previously were unemployed."

The New Deal brought electricity to farm areas and paved dirt roads.

Buildings and schools began to spring up in small communities. All of this was a step in the right direction, Fitzgerald said.

"People began to have more access to other areas," he said. "The New Deal brought Kansas out of the 19th century and into the 20th. It brought us the modern conveniences we take for granted today."

Of all the towns and cities in Kansas, Fitzgerald said, Wichita benefited the most.

The New Deal can be credited with the widening of Broadway and the construction of Morrison Hall at Wichita State University, Marshall Middle School at 1510 Payne, Lawrence-Dumont Stadium, the Wichita Municipal Airport and the Wichita Art Museum.

"There were some projects accomplished under the New Deal that might never have been done," Ellington said. "These projects changed the look of Wichita."

Of particular interest, Ellington said, was the river beautification project. It included the construction of McLean Boulevard and developed the course of the Arkansas River through downtown. That project also removed Ackerman Island from the river channel. The island had previously stretched from Douglas to where the Keeper of the Plains statue stands today.

During the New Deal, married men who had lived in Wichita for at least one year and had no other income were entitled to two days of work each week with one or another of the alphabet agencies. They were guaranteed $2.25 a day in pay.

According to local papers at the time, the WPA financed most of the runways at the airport and many road and bridge projects; created Lake Afton, west of Goddard; built

more than 500 miles of new roads; constructed 14 new buildings and improved 11; and built more than 30,000 lineal feet of levees and embankments for flood control. Altogether, the WPA spent $8.5 million—the equivalent of $150 million today, according to Larry Henry, maintenance engineer for the city's public works department. Those projects were constructed in Wichita between 1935 and 1940 and at one time they employed 3,000 local people.

There was also extensive WPA construction in El Dorado and Augusta as Butler County emerged from the Depression in the late 1930s.

The WPA projects included the Forest Park band shell and McDonald Stadium, both in El Dorado and both still in use.

The WPA also built structures called "appropriate outhouses" that were designed to be sanitary. They had screened vents and were fairly resistant to flies, said Bob Burgess, director of the Butler County Historical Society Museum. There is still one in El Dorado on rental property on South High.

"There was a need for safer outhouses," Burgess said. "People did not associate bad sanitary practices with dysentery."

But the WPA workers in Butler County didn't just build buildings. They also worked on road surfacing in Douglass Township and other parts of southern Butler County, built a dam two miles east of Leon for the Leon water plant, and set out thousands of trees for beautification, according to Jessie Stratford and Lawrence Klintworth, authors of "The Kingdom of Butler." In the museum, several sets of dolls dressed in traditional costumes of various countries are the work of WPA artists.

All in all, Roosevelt's New Deal and the WPA still get praise. And Langsdorf, the new KU grad in 1935, still is grateful.

"WPA provided jobs for a lot of people who were qualified but unable to find jobs," said Langsdorf, now a retired assistant secretary of the Kansas State Historical Society. "I was one of them."

Langsdorf spent two years with the WPA, compiling inventories of county records across the state.

"The WPA had a great deal of impact on the state that was good," he said. "Although the pay was not always great, it was reasonable. I earned $100 a month, which wasn't bad pay in those times."

Buffalo Herds, Grasshopper Plagues and Drunken Soldiers

"When we first got to Wichita we boarded with Old Man Munger. . . . We lived upstairs over the log part of it, and I remember upsetting some water on the floor which was made of cottonwood planks and not very tight and it dripped on Old Man Munger's bald head and he seriously objected."
—E.B. Allen,
one of Wichita's first physicians

Jesse Chisholm

He gave town's business life its start

Wind blows the grass along the site where local historians say Jesse Chisholm opened Wichita's first business, two years after Kansas became a state.

That trading post, started in 1863, was west of where Martin Luther King Jr. Expressway, or I-135, now crosses 18th Street. Rubber Belting and Hose Supply, 1850 Ohio, is the present-day building closest to the spot.

Chisholm operated cabins, a trading post and a corral there until about 1868, when he died from eating rancid bear grease. During that five-year period, he constructed a second post at what is now the Twin Lakes parking lot at 21st and Amidon.

Born in 1805 in eastern Tennessee, Chisholm was the son of a Scottish trader and a Cherokee woman. During the 1830s, when gold was discovered on Cherokee lands in Georgia, the U.S. military uprooted the entire Cherokee nation and drove the people into what is now Oklahoma.

Chisholm traveled with the Cherokees and settled at Fort Gibson, Okla., near Muskogee, where he began trading.

Old newspaper clippings say Chisholm came to the confluence of the Arkansas and Little Arkansas rivers in 1836. He was leading a group of men who were searching for a gold mine, based on an old map they had found that had been published in New Orleans in 1757.

They did not find the mine, but Chisholm remembered the area. Later, when the Wichita Indians asked him to find them a place to settle, he came back to the area and started trading cloth, buttons, sugar, flour and other staples with the Indians in exchange for furs.

Chisholm also conducted trading trips that took him into Indian Territory, now eastern Oklahoma. The trail he used and the Wichita creek along which his first trading post

Jesse Chisholm died in 1868 from eating rancid bear grease.

sat have been named for him.

In 1866, while he was in Leavenworth, Chisholm and J.R. Mead happened to be passing a photographer. Mead persuaded Chisholm to have his photo taken. It was the only photo of Chisholm, according to T.U. Taylor in the book "The Chisholm Trail and Other Routes."

But Mead had another picture of Chisholm.

In the spring of 1868, Chisholm died in Oklahoma from food poisoning caused by eating rancid bear grease that had been cooked in a brass kettle.

"For mountain men, eating bear grease was not that unusual," said Dan Fitzgerald, archivist for the Kansas State Historical Society. "At that time there were still a few small black bear in the area."

Fitzgerald said Chisholm may have viewed the opportunity to eat bear as a treat in an otherwise bland

Jeff Johnston/The Wichita Eagle

Rubber Belting and Hose Supply, 1850 Ohio, is the present-day building closest to the site where Jesse Chisholm opened his trading post, which was Wichita's first business.

diet. "Bear meat was a staple just like buffalo was at that time." The official cause of Chisholm's death was "Cholera morbus." Fitzgerald said Chisholm ate bear on the night before he died. Because of lack of refrigeration or of a way to properly store the meat, it and grease sat overnight in the kettle. When Chisholm ate again, he was poisoned by the bacteria in the grease.

Mead and a group of others saw their friend off in style.

An article from the June 23, 1952, Kansas City Star said: "With the aid of a small keg of Kentucky's best, taken from the center of a barrel of sugar, the men held what Mead called a fitting wake, ending with a salute from their guns."

Chisholm is buried at his last campsite near Johnny Left Hand Spring on the North Canadian River, about six miles north of Geary, Okla.

An inscription on his grave reads: "Jesse Chisholm, born 1805, died March 4, 1868. No one left his home cold or hungry."

Elias Hicks Durfee

Trader peddled the virtues of Wichita

When Elias Hicks Durfee decided to build a trading post in Wichita in the 1860s, Midtown was part of a prairie dotted by buffalo.

Durfee, a Quaker from New York, came to Wichita during the winter of 1867. His trading post, in what now is the 400 block of West Ninth, soon marked the hub of a growing community.

Elias Hicks Durfee started his Wichita trading post in 1867. It was one of several that formed the Great American Fur Co.

He had other trading posts, up and down the Missouri River, through the Dakotas and in Montana. He had licenses to buy furs, robes and hides from Indian tribes such as the Blackfeet, Sioux and Crow.

Durfee and his brother-in-law bought out the Great American Fur Co., and the company was then known as Durfee & Peck. It became the largest fur and robe company in the West.

Durfee did not spend a lot of time at his Wichita trading post. Instead, he stayed in Leavenworth—where he had his headquarters—and relied on managers Phil Ledrick and Milo Kellogg to run local affairs.

Nevertheless, he was the man who promoted the little town.

He had circulars printed which described Wichita, and distributed them to Texas cattlemen, encouraging them to bring their cattle through the town.

Durfee's circulars marked the first time the name Wichita was used on printed material.

The circulars promoted Wichita as "the center of splendid stock country, where stock will thrive six weeks earlier and later than on the line of the Pacific Railroad. It is the natural point where buyer and seller should meet, to their mutual advantage."

Durfee's Wichita post was a stick-picket structure and was said by William Finn, one of Wichita's early settlers, to be the earliest building.

Kos Harris, an early pioneer, wrote in the Nov. 27, 1917, Wichita Eagle that the 25-by-100-foot structure was a U-shaped building with a fence around the open end of the U.

The front was a storehouse for Indian trading goods. The rest was used as a residence and sleeping room. Over the front door was a sign with Durfee's name, the first sign in the city, said Stan Harder, curator of Old Cowtown Museum.

The Wichita post, like Durfee's other posts, was the focal point for Indians, trappers and frontiersmen who brought in hides and furs for trade. The sheer volume of those animal kills was incredible and often marked with efficiency.

In 1868, Durfee told the Leavenworth Daily Conservative about the way the buffalo were killed.

"The buffalo are killed mostly by arrows, as they are not only less expensive, but can be withdrawn and used again," he said. "A large herd is surrounded and gradually driven in together. The stragglers are shot in the liver and will bleed internally in going four or five miles. When the circle is well closed in, the hunters begin to shoot at the heart."

After a successful buffalo hunt, Durfee said, a hunter would be faced with hungry wolves wanting to scavenge buffalo meat. Since wolf fur also was sought after by

A trading post near what now is Ninth and Waco marked the hub of a growing community. The post eventually was destroyed.

was poisoned with strychnine. The wolves, following the buffalo smell, would eat the meat and die.

Sometimes as many as 70 or 80 wolves were killed with a single quarter of meat. Durfee said he had sold as many as 1,200 bottles of strychnine to one man.

Durfee died in September 1874. He was 45 and suffered from kidney disease.

William Greiffenstein, one of Wichita's co-founders, bought Durfee's post in 1869. After 1870, new frame buildings were sprouting up on either side of Main Street, and the older log and sod buildings were ignored.

The post eventually was destroyed, and town founders later said its logs were used in the construction of the First Episcopal Church.

the Eastern fur companies, hunters soon learned how to kill wolves.

Durfee said quarter sections of a buffalo were taken in a wagon or dragged over the prairie to points about 40 rods apart, and the meat

Andrew Greenway

Ferry operator believed in Wichita's potential

Andrew J. Greenway was a man who believed in possibilities.

When he came to the Wichita area in 1868, he almost immediately began writing to newspapers across the state, encouraging people to visit.

Although little is known about Greenway, he was a member of the Five Civilized Tribes, which consists of the Cherokee, Chickasaw, Chocktaw, Creek and Seminole tribes. He was a second lieutenant in the Cherokee Mounted Rifles during the Civil War. Some records indicate he was Indian, while others say he was adopted into tribes.

Whatever the case, Greenway arrived in Kansas in 1852 and learned the Osage language. Then he went into business trading with Indians.

His wife was a full-blooded Cherokee, which was to Greenway's advantage. It helped in being able to communicate with various tribes.

One of the first inhabitants in the

Andrew Greenway operated a ferry.

Wichita area, Greenway operated a ferry across the Arkansas River. The business was lucrative, and Green-

way is reported to have made as much as $50 a day when the river was up. He operated the ferry from 1868 until 1872.

His wife, Lucy, was a charter member in Wichita's first church, First Presbyterian Church.

The Greenway cabin was on what is now the southwest corner of Kellogg and Main.

Greenway's talent for writing established him as one of the area's earliest chroniclers.

Greenway left the Wichita area in the mid-1870s. He later became editor of an Oklahoma newspaper, The Chiefton.

Today, all that remains in Wichita of the Greenway name is a street that runs south along the east bank of the Arkansas River from Harry to Pawnee. The street also extends from Second Street to Central at the bridge. The name is also given to Greenway Manor.

Greenway died in Oklahoma on March 18, 1892.

Camp Beecher

Drunken and bored soldiers sweated it out at military outpost

A field of concrete, dozens of cars and an occasional candy bar wrapper are on the spot where soldiers once shuffled wearily and sweated out the hot Kansas summers in their heavy woolen uniforms.

The Dillons parking lot at 13th and Waco was the site of early Wichita's military outpost from 1868 to 1869.

"It was very much a rudimentary, short-term post," said Mark Alley, a military history buff who has researched the camp and other military sites in Kansas. "There is not one particle of physical evidence left."

During its existence, the camp had three names. It was first known as Camp Butterfield, then as Camp Davidson, and finally, on Oct. 19, 1868, the name was changed to Camp Beecher. First Lt. Frederick Beecher, for whom it was named, had been a hero in the Battle of the Arickaree and was a nephew of

Camp Beecher was built to protect settlers from Indians.

Henry Ward Beecher, an eloquent clergyman.

Although Frederick Beecher was never stationed at the camp, the military still wanted to honor him.

Alley said the camp contained a bakery, company quarters, ammunition building, hospital, guardhouse, post headquarters, wagon park, corral, tents, flagpole, assembly area and other buildings related to military posts.

The camp was built to protect settlers from the Indians.

"But there was some mixed feelings about what the camp's purpose was," Alley said. "It was to offer some frontier protection, but some say it also had some political connections—that is, town developers used it to get more activity into the area."

Usually one infantry company, or about 90 men, was stationed at the camp.

However, the 7th Cavalry also used the camp, which sometimes boosted its numbers by an additional 70 men. During one weeklong period in November 1868, Alley said, the entire 19th Regiment—800 men—camped at the post.

Craig Miner, a history professor at Wichita State University who has written several books and articles

The Dillons parking lot at 13th and Waco used to be part of Camp Beecher, Wichita's military outpost, from 1868 to 1869.

on the American West, said there weren't many activities to keep the soldiers occupied.

"They drank," Miner said. "They didn't fight Indians, so they drank."

Originally, the camp was at the fork of the Arkansas and Little Arkansas rivers, Miner said, but to discourage the troops from going into town to get drunk, the camp was moved to 12th and Jackson and stretched to the 13th and Waco location.

In his book, "Wichita: The Early Years, 1865-80," Miner wrote that discipline at Camp Beecher was almost nonexistent.

"Army officials felt that keeping the soldiers at the post might be more dangerous than an Indian raid, and Camp Beecher was abandoned forever on June 3, 1869," he wrote.

But Ellington said the camp was abandoned because of the times.

"The picture changed so dramatically in just one year," Ellington said. "It had been hostile, and now it was peaceful. We didn't have any Indian attacks here, and a treaty was signed which removed all Indians—the Cheyenne, Arapaho, Apache and Kiowa-Apache—from the Big Arkansas west to Colorado."

Edmund Mosley

His trading post catered to hunters, trappers and Indians

Trees and houses have sprung up in the neighborhood where Edmund H. Mosley first braved the wilds of a buffalo-dotted frontier and built a trading post that catered to hunters, trappers and Indians.

Mosley was the first trader in the Wichita area. In 1857, he constructed a post near where the Osage Trail crossed the Arkansas River, southwest of the intersection at 61st North and Seneca.

He pursued several ventures including trading, tried his hand at farming and sent specimens of animal life to East Coast menageries, circuses and museums.

Although no pictures of Mosley exist, one of the developers of Wichita, J.R. Mead, described Mosley as a large, strong man with blue eyes and locks of black hair hanging to his shoulders.

An article in the October 1896 Eureka Herald, describing the view from the Mosley home next to the trading post, said: "Members of the family could stand in the doorway of the dwelling and look out upon countless herds of buffalo."

Their nearest neighbors lived 18 miles away, the article said.

Mosley spent a great deal of time away from his cabin. During one of those absences, a group of Indians raided the family and the trading post.

"Such occurrences as these convinced the Mosleys that they had selected a home too far out on the frontier, and they became settlers of Greenwood County and lived for several years on Bachelor Creek," according to the 1896 Eureka Herald article. The Wichita trading post burned within a year after the Mosleys left the area.

Mosley was active in public affairs and was elected the Greenwood County surveyor in 1863. During the early 1860s, one of the curiosities in the county was a herd of young buffalo that he kept on his farm. Mosley later took the herd to the East Coast for exhibition.

The frontier eventually called to Mosley again, and in 1871 he began developing a ranch in the southern part of Comanche County, near Kiowa.

An article from the Newton Kansan, dated Sept. 12, 1872, described an attack by a band of Osage Indians on Mosley at his ranch.

"A party of whites had come to the ranch that day in search of a missing comrade and were going to water their ponies, when they saw a large band of warriors dashing up along the timber towards the ranch," the article said.

Laura Rauch/The Wichita Eagle

Edmund Mosley, the Wichita area's first trader, is commemorated in this stone tablet near 61st North and Seneca.

"Mosley remarked that they were Black Dog's band, and as they came up firing, they fired a volley completely riddling Mosley with bullets and driving the rest of the party into the ranch."

A rapid exchange of bullets followed, and the Indians retreated into the brush. When the fight was over, Mosley and 15 Indians lay dead, along with 20 horses.

What remains in Wichita of the early-day trader is a downtown street that bears his name and a small stone tablet on the site of his trading post.

Eli Waterman

Wichita's first landowner aided Texas' liberation

Eli Waterman doesn't get much recognition in most Wichita history accounts, but he was instrumental in the city's having a history.

A member of the troops who captured Santa Anna during Texas' fight for independence, he was the first landowner in what became Wichita.

When he came to Wichita, Waterman had already been hardened by the Kansas prairie. He had previously settled in Marion County and was a highly respected merchant.

He was born in Rhode Island in 1814. Newspaper articles say he left home at 19 to become a sailor, but within four years he was fighting in Texas. In 1836, he was among the 900 men serving under Sam Houston in Texas' fight for independence from Mexico. Armed with squirrel rifles and bowie knives, they overran Santa Anna and 1,200 Mexican soldiers during the battle of San Jacinto.

In 1868, when Waterman was 54, he came to the Wichita area and homesteaded a quarter section of land, bounded by the Arkansas River and what now are Waco, Central and Douglas.

There were about 30 people living in Wichita. Wichita was a small village with only a few cabins. It wasn't legal to own land until after 1870, but somehow Waterman filed for a claim.

When Waterman did file for land, William Finn was an early surveyor for what are now Butler and Sedgwick counties. In September 1926, Finn's account of how Waterman became the first legal land-

Eli Waterman's property was at the corner of Central and Waco. Only about 30 people were living in the area when he started homesteading the land in 1868.

owner in Wichita was published in "Community Life and Development." The property was on Osage Indian land, and Waterman paid a $200 filing fee for it.

"No one, in 1869, thought the main city would be on Waterman's land," Finn wrote. "Mr. Waterman was the first man to prove his quarter section and get a clear title from Uncle Sam."

Finn said that when Waterman's claim became legal, William Greiffenstein—the man historians consider the "Father of Wichita"—made arrangements to buy 80 acres of it. But at that same time, D.S. Munger was interested in beginning a town. The day after Waterman filed his homesteading claim, Munger also filed for land, bounded by what now are Central,

Ninth, Broadway and Waco.

Greiffenstein wanted the land he bought to be the original town site, not an addition, and pleaded with Finn to survey the land.

Finn did, and Greiffenstein's newly bought land, along with Munger's, became the original town site.

Waterman continued to own land in Wichita until 1876, when he and his family left for Arizona.

While in Wichita, though, Waterman was a merchant and ran a general merchandise store on the first or second hundred block of North Main. The townspeople always called him "Father Waterman." He was an elder statesman and looked upon as the original pioneer.

Waterman, at age 87, died in Craig, Ariz., on March, 22, 1901.

William Finn

In an old Army dugout, he saw outline of city's first school

In a way, there isn't much that William Finn isn't credited with doing. As a surveyor, educator and church organizer, Finn's ingenuity came in handy for Wichita's early residents.

Finn is credited with organizing the city's first school, in an abandoned Army dugout on land that is now the southeast corner of 12th and Jackson. He also organized a group of Presbyterians who held religious services there, and later became a charter member of First Presbyterian Church.

But it was Finn's surveying instruments that changed Wichita from a nondescript smattering of shacks on the Arkansas River to a city built systematically.

He was Wichita's first surveyor.

Finn was born on July 4, 1848, in Brooklyn, N.Y. His mother died when he was young, and he was placed in an orphanage. To earn his keep there, he sold newspapers. When he was 12, he was placed on an orphan train and taken to Rockford, Ill., where he worked on neighborhood farms.

Finn was a drummer on the Union side during the last three months of the Civil War. After the war, he heard about Kansas. In 1869, he decided to explore.

His first glimpse of Wichita was nine shacks on a cattle trail.

Not long after his arrival in Wichita, Finn came upon Camp Beecher, an abandoned Army outpost. He looked at one of the dugouts made

William Finn described the old Army dugout as "quite commodious."

by soldiers a year earlier and cleaned it as best as he could.

"I found it quite commodious, with a fireplace and dormer windows on the south side of the roof," he wrote to his future wife, Mary Hazen of Andover, Mass.

In another letter, he wrote: "My old church, the Second Congregational of Rockford, Illinois, has sent me the two dozen hymn books. They help a lot. We use them both in Sunday School and day school. I have a tuning fork so we manage to get started."

In his school there were no desks

and only a few benches.

Finn sent to Topeka for a shipment of books, slates and tablets, expecting the pupils to reimburse him. However, in several instances the parents refused to buy the books and insisted their children use books that the families had already purchased.

That first year, school began Nov. 1 and ended three months later with Finn $50 in debt. He was bailed out by one of his friends and patrons—J.R. Mead.

Mead also helped Finn purchase a surveying outfit, and Finn then left the teaching profession.

His first job as a surveyor was to plat Wichita. He was short of materials, so he used a heavy manila sugar sack as paper and a counter in William Greiffenstein's store as a drawing board.

As he was laying out plats for the area now bounded by Central, Douglas, Waco and Broadway, Finn didn't have a surveyor's chain. He relied on a rope.

Old newspaper accounts say it laid out in a heavy rain, causing it to stretch and shrink. As a result, the lots on the north side of Douglas Avenue are 14 feet deeper than the lots on the south side.

Finn died from an infection of his thyroid gland on July 19, 1929. He was 81 years old. A three-story elementary school was built in 1929 at 520 W. 25th and named in honor of Finn. It was closed in 1974; the building was razed.

Fred Augustus Sowers

Frontier editor founded town's first newspaper

When Fred Augustus Sowers first came to Wichita, he experienced life as only a frontier journalist could.

He ate meals, for instance, that featured sowbelly and beans and

boiled coffee prepared over a dinky little fire made of buffalo chips and cottonwood brush.

And to think people later said he was a gentleman.

Sowers came to Wichita in 1870

with William Bloomfield Hutchinson from Leavenworth, where they had worked on the Leavenworth Times. Sowers was an editorial writer, Hutchinson a printer.

The two men started the Wichita

Fred Sowers helped start the first newspaper in the area, The Wichita Vidette.

Vidette, the first newspaper in the Arkansas River Valley. In the first issue, printed Aug. 12, 1870, Sowers said:

"This is the name of our paper. The word is from the French, who spell it Vedette. It means an outpost, or picket, or rather, 'sentinel on horse back,' as Webster hath it. As we conceive ourselves to be the sentinel or picket of journalism in southwestern Kansas, we claim the right to spell the word as we see proper and therefore print it Vidette. Of course we expect some smart aleck of a quill-driver will discover a mare's nest as soon as our title strikes his eye; and we expect him to go for us on what he will imagine to be very bad orthography, or at best a misprint, but we don't care a continental.

" 'Vidette' is the name of our paper, and we purpose having it known as such."

Sowers was born in Canton, Ohio, in 1838. He fought on the Union side during the Civil War. He arrived in eastern Kansas in 1864 and started work as an attorney in Leavenworth. After two years, he began writing for the Leavenworth Times.

Early in 1870, business leaders from Wichita began recruiting the editor of the Times, Joe Clarke, to set up a newspaper. Clarke sent Sowers instead.

A printing press was hauled by wagon from Fort Harker in Kanapolis.

Sowers was with the Vidette for one year before he sold his portion to Hutchinson. In 1872, he co-founded The Beacon with David Millison and continued operating the newspaper for four more years. He then sold his interests and dealt in real estate and loans.

Near the time of his death on Feb. 4, 1918, The Wichita Eagle reported of Sowers' early years as a journalist:

"Wichita was then on the extreme edge of civilization. Outlawry was rampant. The toughest characters in the West infested the hamlet. It required brave editors to face the situation, but Sowers and Hutchinson not only had moral but physical courage, and they measured up to the duty of true spokesmen of the better life of the community."

The article later said, "Mr. Sowers had a very pleasant style of writing. He had a lively strain of humor and for that reason his stories had a strong charm for the pioneer."

Sowers chronicled not only the news but the history of early Wichita.

He talked about the number of cattle that were driven on the Chisholm Trail, the shootings at Delano. He wrote about people who he bumped into on the streets.

In 1918, Sowers died in his home at 875 Spaulding. He was 80 years old.

The Sowers Alternative School at 2400 Wassall is named for him. And although his home still stands, it has been incorporated into the building of Church of the Savior.

The Wichita Beacon

Cowboys made the news and bought the papers

The 117-year-old tradition of The Wichita Beacon came to an end Sept. 7, 1989, when its name was dropped from the masthead of The Wichita Eagle.

The Beacon boasted a proud legacy but was often overshadowed by its competitor, The Eagle.

The first paper in Wichita's history was the Wichita Vidette, founded in 1870 by F.A. Sowers. In October 1872, Sowers and David Millison started The Beacon, which was the first daily newspaper in the Arkansas Valley.

During the first few weeks as a daily, The Beacon flourished.

The Texas cattle drives were on, and thousands of longhorns were moved along a trail that is now Douglas Avenue. At night, hundreds of cowboys crowded the streets. There were killings, shootings and trials, making plenty of news and plenty of patronage for the newspaper.

But when the cattle drives ended, news became scarce, and The Beacon switched to weekly

The first Beacon Building was a two-story structure on the southeast corner of Second and Main.

publication. It remained a weekly until 1884, when it became a daily again. The paper was bought in 1874 by Frank Smith and Frank Fischer, who built the first Beacon Building, a two-story structure on the southeast corner of Second and Main.

In 1875, W.C. "Cap" White of Kingman bought one-third interest in the paper, and the growing Beacon was moved to the second floor of 112 E. Douglas.

It moved again in 1883 to 121 N. Market.

During the next three decades the paper changed hands several times. In 1907, Henry J. Allen

bought it. He later became a Kansas governor and an appointee to the U.S. Senate, and he switched the paper's politics to Republican.

In 1910, Allen built a 10-story Beacon Building at 114 S. Main. It was hailed as Wichita's first skyscraper.

The paper changed hands again in 1928 when it was purchased by Max and Louis Levand. In 1954, The Beacon moved into a new two-story structure with railroad trackage at 825 E. Douglas.

The Levand family maintained the paper until 1960, when The Eagle bought assets and stock of The Beacon Newspaper Corp. and be-

gan publishing in the afternoon The Wichita Evening Eagle and Beacon.

After the Beacon's building was remodeled in 1961, the city's two papers—The Eagle and The Beacon—were published at 825 E. Douglas. Then, in 1973, the two papers were sold to Ridder Publications. In 1980, the two papers were merged into The Wichita Eagle-Beacon. The paper was redesigned and many features and sections were added. One of the additions was Neighbors, which carried some of the features The Beacon traditionally carried, such as the Daily Record.

Milo Kellogg

City's first postmaster got the mail out

Local townspeople used to say that when Milo Kellogg, Wichita's first postmaster, delivered the mail, he fit all of it into his hat or hip pockets.

Kellogg became Wichita's first civilian postmaster in 1868. He was born in Marion, N.Y. A Union soldier in the Civil War, Kellogg was held in the Confederate Andersonville Prison in Georgia. After the war, the 27-year-old came to Wichita to manage the Durfee Trading Post in what is now the 400 block of West Ninth.

While at the post, Kellogg came up with the idea for postal delivery.

In those days, mail was delivered

to Wichita by anyone who happened to be heading west from Towanda. When the mail arrived at the Durfee Trading Post, Kellogg would fit it into his hat or pockets and deliver it to the appropriate people.

For convenience's sake he would take it to them, or residents would pick it up at the trading post.

In 1868, Kellogg established Wichita as a federally designated post office, complete with reliable, regular service.

Milo Kellogg would fit mail into his hat or pockets.

A drawing shows an earlier version of Kellogg Traditional Magnet School at Kellogg and Laura. The school named after Kellogg was built in 1890.

By the 1870s the town had grown, and Kellogg left the trading post and postal service to become a partner in one of the town's leading grocery stores, Kellogg and Jocelyn, on North Main. He also was the register of deeds.

During the summer of 1874, Kansas was plagued by grasshoppers, which destroyed that year's crops and gardens. Wichita and the surrounding areas were particularly hard hit. That winter, townspeople organized a local aid society, and Kellogg became a government agent for distributing the food to the needy. In the spring of 1875, The Wichita Eagle reported that Kellogg traveled to Fort Riley and back to issue food.

"The grasshoppers were like a tornado of bugs coming through here," Ellington said. "They ate all the laundry hanging out on lines, all the crops, anything green. The people were in dire straits. Kellogg was the appointed one for acquiring foodstuffs for local people and farmers. He was a very trusted, likable individual."

In 1883, Kellogg left Wichita for Kingman, where he became a real estate agent and loan proprietor. He and his family later moved to Colorado Springs and then to California. He died in Fresno in 1920.

Kellogg Avenue, one of Wichita's major east-west thoroughfares, was named after him in the 1870s. And, in 1890 a school named after Kellogg was built at the intersection of Kellogg and Laura.

D.S. Munger

His log cabin soon became an early hotel

In the spring of 1868, Darius Sales Munger arrived in Wichita.

As one of the representatives in the Wichita Town Co., Munger was to file a legal claim on a 160-acre plot suitable for town lots. The Munger development took in the area now bounded by Murdock, Ninth, Waco and Wichita Street.

Munger accomplished that goal, said Stan Harder, curator of Old Cowtown Museum. Munger also joined with William Greiffenstein,

The house that Darius Sales Munger built was the only structure in early Wichita that had a shingle roof. He hauled logs for it and mixed his own mortar and plaster.

Darius Sales Munger was Wichita's second postmaster and one of its incorporators.

two years later, in incorporating Wichita.

In a paper called "The Munger House 1869-1874," Harder said that after Munger arrived in the new settlement, he started work on a log cabin, retrieving cottonwood logs from an island in the Arkansas River. He mixed his own mortar and plaster from river sand and made lime by burning clamshells found along the river. He then mixed the concoction with the hair of buffalo and used it in constructing his house.

Within a year, the Munger House was standing at what is now the southwest corner of Ninth and Waco. It soon became a hotel for new arrivals in the community.

Charles C. Allen, in a manuscript on the E.B. Allen family, wrote, "When we first got to Wichita we boarded with Old Man Munger. . . . We lived upstairs over the log part of it, and I remember upsetting some water on the floor which was made of cottonwood planks and not very tight and it dripped on Old Man Munger's bald head and he seriously objected." E.B. Allen was one of Wichita's first physicians and later became the first mayor.

In a Wichita Eagle article, James R. Mead pointed out that the Munger House was in the center of the new village on a dirt street that Munger later would name Waco Avenue. Mead noted that the house was the only structure in town that had a shingle roof, the rest all having dirt roofs.

In 1870, Munger became Wichita's second postmaster, after Milo Kellogg, who posted mail from the Durfee Trading Post. Munger moved the post office to his hotel.

"Munger was a model postmaster," Harder said in his paper. "He knew the name and face of every patron of his office and the quarter section he lived on and just when he took it. But the host of immigrants that poured into the country that summer was too much for the old man; he couldn't remember them all so he resigned."

As more and more people arrived in the area, buildings sprang up not only in Munger's development but also in a development started by Greiffenstein, around what is now the intersection of First and Main. When the town was incorporated in 1870, the two developments were merged.

Greiffenstein and Munger could see that by working against one another, the town wouldn't grow. That's how Central Avenue got its name, because it was the central dividing point between the two areas of land.

Harder said that after the town's incorporation, the Munger development became known as Old Town. It was identified as that until the turn of the century, when the area was redeveloped and the old buildings were removed.

"For years, citizens referred to Old Town as that log development that Munger developed," Harder said.

The Munger House still stands but has been moved to Old Cowtown Museum.

Andrew Fabrique

Pioneer doctor's name lives on

I n Wichita's medical community, Andrew Fabrique is a legend.

From 1870 to 1911, Fabrique was a pioneer doctor. He was one of the first staff doctors of what is now St. Francis Regional Medical Center.

"He was a spark plug. Oh, they still tell stories of Fabrique's practice," said Dean Schwartz, director of employee health services at St. Francis, who worked on writing a centennial history of the medical center's staff.

Schwartz said the medical center still has the Fabrique Society, an organization of staff and alumni that promotes medical advances.

Fabrique never formerly attended medical school. His knowledge came from working with doctors, especially those from the

Andrew Fabrique worked as a physician but never attended medical school.

Civil War. Fabrique was 19 when the war broke out, and he enlisted as a soldier with the Union forces.

In April 1862, his left arm was shattered at the elbow during the Battle of Shiloh. The arm eventually healed, but it was weaker than his right. After the war, he went to Mexico with Gen. Phillip H. Sheridan to help overthrow the Mexican

Today, St. Francis Regional Medical Center stands where Andrew Fabrique practiced medicine as a staff doctor during his days in Wichita.

Gregory Drezdzon/The Wichita Eagle

government. The Americans suffered from yellow fever at Vera Cruz, and Fabrique, although not a doctor, helped by tending to the sick.

After the war, Fabrique went to Illinois, where he and his brother, Dudley, purchased a drugstore in Aurora. He attended lectures at Rush Medical College and helped an elderly doctor by making house calls and filling prescriptions.

Fabrique came to Wichita in 1870 and began his medical career with the city's first doctor, E.B. Allen. The Wichita doctors' medical practice stretched north to Newton, east to the Walnut River, south to what is now the Oklahoma state line, and west into Kingman and Pratt counties.

Fabrique lived at the northwest corner of Central and Broadway. His medical office was in the 200 block of East Douglas. When he began working with St. Francis Hospital, the building was where the medical center now stands, at 929 N. St. Francis.

By 1901, Kansas had passed a law requiring all doctors who had not graduated from a medical school to register, Schwartz said.

"Fabrique said he was as good a practitioner as anybody else and wouldn't do anything about registering."

Rather than see a favored physician on the wrong side of the law, Schwartz said, some of Fabrique's interns, who had come from Northwestern University, banded together and persuaded university officials to grant Fabrique a medical degree.

He was awarded the degree in 1901 and traveled to Chicago to receive it.

"Through the years he was considered probably the No. 1 medicine man in the community," Ellington said. "His contribution was not only locally to his patients but to the men he trained in medicine. He was looked upon with a great admiration and respect."

Fabrique died in 1928.

E.B. and Joe Allen

Brothers brought law and medicine to town

For two decades, the Allen brothers were a formidable pair in determining Wichita's medical and political climate.

The eldest of the two, E.B., in 1869 became Wichita's first physician and in 1870 became coroner. He also was its first elected mayor, in 1871, and later served in several state offices. His brother, Joe, was the city's first pharmacist and served as mayor during 1887 and 1888.

E.B. situated his medical practice at 108 E. Douglas, which is near where One Main Place is now. Joe opened his pharmacy, where he sold oil, kerosene, herbs and drugs in the same building.

Of the two, E.B. was the most well-known.

He was unique because of his three responsibilities as mayor, physician and coroner. He was an intelligent individual, which probably made him stand out.

E.B. Allen Memorial Hospital, which now houses the University of Kansas School of Medicine-Wichita, was named for him. The medical school moved into the hospital at 1010 N. Kansas in 1977.

"The naming of the hospital was a fitting tribute to the pioneer phy-

One Main Place, at the northeast corner of Main and Douglas, stands about where E.B. Allen established his medical practice and his brother, Joe, had his pharmacy.

sicians who came out on the Plains," said William Reals, the school's vice chancellor. "He was dedicated to the care of people from the start."

E.B. Allen died in April 1908 at age 72. The Wichita Eagle reported that he had been paralyzed two

E.B. Allen was Wichita's first elected mayor, its first coroner and its first physician.

Joe Allen was Wichita's first pharmacist and the city's mayor in 1887 and 1888.

months before.

"The news of Dr. Allen's death was received with great sorrow by his many friends in the city. He was one of the most prominent of the old residents of the city," the paper said.

Although Joe didn't climb the state political ladder as his brother did, he still was considered prominent in the Wichita community. Upon his death in August 1903, crowds turned out.

"An unusually large number of people were present at the funeral of J.P. Allen at the home at 353 N. Lawrence yesterday afternoon, testifying to the esteem in which this worthy man was held by the people of Wichita," reported an Aug. 21, 1903, copy of The Wichita Weekly Beacon.

Park City

Town didn't stand a chance against Wichita

From the first, Park City didn't stand a chance.

Part of the reason was that it never really was a natural meeting place for Indians, traders or politicians. But the real reason was that it couldn't compete with Wichita and lost out in establishing itself as the place for the county seat, railroads and cattle drives.

"It was a case of two western towns that battled one another in a high competition for survival," Ellington said. "Wichita came out the winner but Park City had great dreams."

The dream of establishing a town called Park City began in the early 1870s. It was located off the Arkansas River seven miles west of Valley Center. The town was never more than a few cabins, settled for 10 years and then returned to the prairie. It failed to thrive because the town never established any hardcore leaders.

Also, Wichita out-promoted Park City.

As was the case with Wichita, the land at Park City was originally owned by the Osage Indians until Oct. 22, 1870, when the federal government relocated the tribe to Indian Territory, now known as Oklahoma.

However, some white settlement attempts were made in the late 1850s. C.C. Arnold came from Coffey County in 1857 and joined a party of settler-hunters. Arnold, along with Robert Dunlap, Jack Carey, Bob DeRacken, Thompson Crawford, Edward Mosley and another man named Maxley, built cabins on the site that became Park City and cultivated some land.

The men made a living by capturing buffalo calves for exhibition in Eastern parks and traveling menageries. They were there about a year before they left.

"They came out here to test the waters in trading, and it wasn't as lucrative as it could have been," Ellington said. "And it was so dangerous out here at that time, that's

The saloon at right in the background of an 1871 photo is now a museum at Sedgwick; it and a few buildings were all of what was the original Park City.

probably what really discouraged them. This was very raw country then."

In 1860, John Ross brought his wife and children to the area and built a cabin and started farming. When his horses were stolen, he and his hired hand left to recover them but never returned. His wife and children quickly departed for the East Coast.

Until 1869, the land at Park City remained unsettled, with the exception of a farmer named William Jewett. That year and the next, there were heated contests between Park City and Wichita over which town would have a railroad and be the county seat.

Park City secured its railroad before Wichita. However, it remained on paper while the Wichita boys had an actual railroad by 1872.

The Park City townspeople then campaigned for the Sedgwick County seat in a heated election. When the spring of 1870 election was over, there was some question once the ballots were counted.

After the election, some people found some ballots for the Park City cause in the river. It wasn't enough to offset the election, but it was believed that some skullduggery was going on.

The final blow to Park City came in 1871 with Texas cattle drives. The Park City residents tried unsuc-

cessfully to lure cattlemen to their town, but failed when four of Wichita's business leaders—N.A. English, Mike Meagher, J.M. Steele and J.R. Mead—rode out to the herds and persuaded the cowboys to pass through Wichita.

The town site was soon abandoned; many of the buildings were removed or left to fall down. The land became farmland.

In the 1950s, a new Park City was created when land at 61st North was purchased by two Wichita developers, Don Morris and Eddie Zongker, for residential development.

Cattle Drives

Bitter rivalry sprang up over herds on the Chisholm Trail

When city founders gathered in the late 1860s to shape the future of Wichita, power and politics played heavily in their discussions.

At issue was a bitter rivalry with Park City over cattle on the Chisholm Trail.

Beginning in 1868 and continuing for almost a decade, the Chisholm Trail carried thousands of cattle from Texas to Abilene by way of Wichita. And until the railroad arrived in Wichita in 1872, the trail extended north through Park City, which set the towns at odds.

The original Park City was seven miles west of Valley Center on the Arkansas River and received its name from the number of parks townspeople wanted to establish.

Park City residents tried to outwit Wichitans in luring cowboys off the dusty Chisholm Trail. They told the cowboys the waters running through Wichita were poisonous to cattle.

But once cattleman started making Park City their stop, Wichita leaders N.A. English, Mike Meagher, J.R. Mead and J.M. Steele got wind of it.

What took place is that the Wichita men rode out and told the cattle-

Thousands of cattle were driven through Wichita on the Chisholm Trail for almost a decade beginning in 1868. Wichita was one of the major stations on the trail from Texas to Abilene.

men it was strictly a hoax. The cattlemen were then offered financial incentives for stopping in Wichita.

Their ploy worked.

And as soon as Wichita had secured the cattle, the four horsemen's next move was to bring the railroad to town.

In April 1872, the Wichita and Southwestern, a spur off what now is the Santa Fe Railway, came to

Wichita. The loading pens for the cattle were a block south of where Waterman and Santa Fe now intersect.

With the cattle came promoters. One of Wichita's most notorious and flamboyant was Abel Head "Shanghai" Pierce. Pierce is credited with introducing Brahman cattle in the United States.

Shortly after the Civil War, records indicate, Pierce was a partner in the Pierce-Sullivan Pasture Co. in Texas, which had more than 250,000 acres of land and sent thousands of cattle up the northern trails to Kansas.

"He drove cattle to Wichita and sold them here and was listed as one of the cattlemen in town in some of the issues of The Wichita Eagle," said the late Waldo Koop, a local historian. "He came here to get the best sale price he could get. He didn't trust his help to do it for him."

As a Wichita cattle dealer, Pierce's reputation intimidated his peers.

In his book, "Cattle Trade of the West and Southwest," first published in 1874, Joseph McCoy wrote that Pierce dealt seriously

"Shanghai" Pierce was one of the most flamboyant cattle promoters.

with people who angered him. His enemies died soon after crossing him and "were seen hanging to the limbs of a dead tree as human fruit."

The Wichita Eagle reported on Dec. 20, 1900, that Shanghai was dead:

"When he whispered, the whole town heard him. When he laughed, the earth trembled. The roar of the ocean was like the music of a harp compared with his voice when he shouted. He was a human megaphone. Large, long and bony. A distinguished figure in every record, and that is the reason he was called 'Shanghai.' "

The last of the Texas cattle drives was in 1876 when the state quarantine laws were enforced.

Doc Lewellen

Trader-sheriff helped build the city by barter

Doc Lewellen didn't always make money from the trading post he bought from Jesse Chisholm in 1868, but he did conduct a hefty trade in furs, fish and firewood.

When he first took over the business, he bartered. He would trade for items in his operations, such as furs and pelts and foodstuffs.

Lewellen's store drew people to the Wichita area and eventually allowed them to establish a town.

Lewellen was born in 1826 in Pennsylvania. Old newspaper clippings said that his parents named him "Zadok," after the biblical priest under David who brought the ark of the covenant back to Jerusalem. As Lewellen grew older, he didn't care for the name; he rejected the first syllable, and changed the second to "Doc." Lewellen's descendants, however, claim that his birth name was simply "Doc," and that's how he was known throughout his life.

In 1856, Lewellen came to Butler County and settled in Chelsea, a town now covered by El Dorado Lake. While there, Lewellen erected a stone house and became sheriff. In 1868, he bought the trading post

Doc Lewellen's store spurred the city's growth.

from Chisholm at what is now 18th Street and I-135 in Wichita. Chisholm then left for Oklahoma and died shortly thereafter.

But Lewellen stayed in the area, and his trade flourished.

His ledger books indicate the items most traded were canned apples and oysters in barrels.

He sold needles, bricks, whiskey, medicine, groceries, clothing and hardware. In trade, he accepted eggs, butter, lard, pigs, beef and vegetables.

Lewellen contributed to the early settlement of Wichita but eventually returned to Butler County. Before he did, his eldest daughter, Hannah, became the first Wichita bride. His 5-year-old son, Albert, was the first person buried in Highland Cemetery.

The only known photograph of Lewellen was taken in the mid-1860s by a photographer who specialized in taking pictures of Indian traders. Old newspaper accounts of the photo say the photographer did not allow Lewellen to dress up or comb his hair for the photo.

Lewellen died in Butler County in 1901.

"At the time, he settled on the edge of civilization," Ellington said.

"You can imagine the wilderness out here. There was danger. Yet, as more people came he became a very active man in city government, school boards, and was sheriff of Butler County. He rates quite high as one of the key players in the early development out here."

Grasshopper Invasion

Insects devoured clothing, crops and hogs

When grasshoppers came through Sedgwick County, people were devastated and helpless.

The invasion was first reported Aug. 5, 1874, when residents woke to clouds of swarming grasshoppers. There was an incessant buzzing, crackling and rasping sound, similar to the sound a prairie fire makes, according to news reports of the day. The ground was 2 to 3 inches deep in grasshoppers, and it shone like silver dollars in the sun.

"Sedgwick County, Kansas, was more thoroughly overrun than any other county in the state," said Linda Newland, former government documents librarian for the Kansas State Historical Society. "The inhabitants were eaten out of farm and home. Every green thing was destroyed."

The hordes of migratory grasshoppers were caused by a drought that had affected the Great Plains for several years, said Leroy Brooks, extension entomologist for Kansas State University. In times of prolonged rains, cloudiness or high humidity, the insects succumb to bacterial and fungus diseases.

"Grasshoppers are dry-weather pests," Brooks said. "These populations originated on millions of acres of grassland during the dry weather."

The species of grasshopper that invaded Kansas, *Melanoplus spretus*, was a long-winged insect, Brooks said. It began to die out after the summer of 1874, and "by the turn of the century it was gone. It has never been seen since."

Most of the swarms migrated to Kansas from the plains of Montana, Wyoming and Colorado.

Once in Sedgwick County, the grasshoppers stripped the trees of their leaves. The grasshoppers ate all the garden vegetables, even on-

In 1874, when Wichita had a plague of grasshoppers, Ohio donated food and clothing; when floods hit Ohio 10 years later, Wichitans sent 31 carloads of grain.

ions underground. Clothes hanging outside to dry were eaten, and locomotives lost traction from grasshoppers on the tracks. One farmer near Wichita reported his hogs' noses had been destroyed by the grasshoppers.

The grasshoppers often stayed in one location for as long as three days before moving on. Once in flight, Newland said, they could travel 40 miles in a day.

The Kansas Legislature had a special session to seek relief for hungry families throughout the state. President Ulysses S. Grant ordered the U.S. Army to donate more than 10,000 coats, 8,000 blankets and 20,000 boots and shoes to Kansas families.

It became a political issue in Wichita on who needed blankets and relief. Political, in the sense of who qualified, Ellington said. "There was the belief that some seeking assistance didn't need it and those others who did, weren't getting it.

"It was a recession for us," Ellington said. "It hurt us very badly at that time. The crops failed, and it was another year before people here could plant grain to recover losses."

In September 1874, Marshall Murdock, founding editor of The Wichita Eagle, wrote about the grasshopper:

"With one of his ends he devours the substance of the people, with the other he probagates (sic) his vile species in small holes in the ground in little bags of fifty eggs at a single wiggle, darn him. His appetite is only exceeded by his unholy passions. . . . Collectively, they come like the condemned legions that fell with Satan into the brimstone lake. No grasshopper ever died before his fullest time.

"If all the hard words in the dictionary and all the mean epithets of all tongues were stretched out in a sentence a mile long and that sentence boiled down into a single word, that word would be 'damn,' and that's what we think of the grasshopper."

Gunslingers, Saloon Keeps and Thieves

"I shall have the sheriff read the riot act to you people and give you 15 minutes to leave town, and then if you are not gone, will order the sheriff to summon a posse comitatus and arrest the lot of you."
—Judge "Tiger Bill" Campbell

"Tiger Bill" Campbell

Frontier judge stood his ground

"Tiger Bill" Campbell didn't take guff from anybody.

As one of Wichita's earliest judges, he knew the frontier and the way of life that came with it.

Once, when he heard about a plot to murder him, he announced in his courtroom that he knew of it and then revealed the route he would be walking to and from his office for the next few days.

He even said that if any man wanted to fight it out with a six-shooter, he was ready. The would-be killer never appeared.

"He was a little on the crotchety side," Ellington said.

Campbell was born Feb. 18, 1845, at Stanford, Ky. He fought as a sergeant major for the Union during the Civil War. He married after the war and came to the Wichita area in 1872. He was appointed district judge shortly after that. His jurisdiction took in Sedgwick, Butler, Sumner, Howard, Greenwood and Cowley counties.

An article in The Wichita Eagle said that Campbell "jogged from county to county on horseback or drove a horse and buggy through the blizzards of winter or the heat of summer to open his sessions of court."

He opened his first court in Wichita in a room in the Occidental Hotel in 1872.

When residents in Butler County were arguing over where to place the county seat—El Dorado or Augusta—Campbell addressed a riotous crowd of 125 armed men who had gathered in Augusta in preparation for heading to El Dorado to take the county books. He had only a gun containing eight loads.

Campbell delivered this ultimatum when asked what he would do if they took the books:

"I shall have the sheriff read the riot act to you people and give you 15 minutes to leave town, and then if you are not gone, will order the sheriff to summon a posse comitatus and arrest the lot of you."

What he didn't know was that standing behind him were 80 armed men from El Dorado waiting to protect him and the county books.

Campbell earned the name "Tiger Bill" because he was so active in anti-saloon work. The name was applied after he rebuffed threats on his life.

Campbell and his wife, Mary, lived at 807 Gilman. She died in 1915. When the two were married in 1869, Campbell said, his father-in-law told him:

"I like you all right, like your politics; I think you have a future promise amounting to something, but you have nothing in the world

On horseback or in his buggy, "Tiger Bill" Campbell traveled "through the blizzards of winter or the heat of summer to open his sessions of court."

but your brain (and I don't know how long that will last), and I don't want to see my daughter go to the washtub."

Years later, Campbell told a reporter: "That's just where she did go, and she didn't mind it a bit."

Campbell died in March 1936. He was 91 years old.

Henry Clay Sluss

A livery stable was his courtroom

Henry Clay Sluss didn't like publicity.

"I was told of the death of Henry C. Sluss, one of the first thoughts which came to me was that I had never known anyone in Wichita, with his grace of letters, who was as reluctant to put himself

into print as Henry C. Sluss," wrote Victor Murdock in The Wichita Eagle of Aug. 5, 1926.

The reason, Murdock surmised, was that "Henry Sluss, of all men, could not tolerate verbosity," though he "declined at all times to be uninteresting."

At his death, Sluss was remembered by Wichitans for what he had contributed to the city: a flourishing law practice and a deep love of culture.

Sluss fought as a private in the Union Army during the Civil War and came to Wichita from Tuscola,

Ill., in 1870. He stopped his wagon at what is now College Hill and surveyed the valley and small village below.

He is said to have turned to his teamster and cried out: "This royal infant, yet in its cradle, contains for Kansas a thousand blessings, which time shall bring to ripeness."

It is not known what the teamster replied.

In an hour, Sluss had reached Wichita's only hotel—the Buckhorn—on the northeast corner of what is now Ninth and Waco, and settled into the frontier life.

He established himself as one of Wichita's early attorneys. In 1870 and 1871, he argued his clients' cases in the upper story of a livery stable. His law office was in a storeroom on North Main.

Before he located a home of his own, Sluss slept on the floor of the D.S. Munger house and waited on tables to pay for his board. One of his first cases was settling the estate of a man who was hanged by a mob for being a horse thief.

As the town grew, so did Sluss' reputation as an attorney. He was elected county attorney, then district judge, and was appointed to serve on the U.S. Court of Land Claims.

When the United States took land from Mexico, Sluss was responsible for defining whether huge tracts of land in New Mexico were public or private.

His peers praised him. Chester Long, a retired president of the American Bar Association in Wich-

Henry Clay Sluss was "exceedingly handsome" and a "graceful dancer."

ita, said at the time of Sluss' death:

"Until he retired from practice a few years ago, Henry C. Sluss was the acknowledged leader of the Wichita bar. He had no rival. Years ago he was a district judge and a good one. He had served as a state senator. As a member of the Spanish land claims court he made a splendid record in clearing the titles to lands in the West which had been clouded by Mexican land grants.

"For several years he has not practiced, but the older members of the bar always acknowledged his

leadership and enjoyed delightful personal relations with him."

In many ways, Sluss was an enigma for the frontier town. After he died, The Wichita Eagle wrote about him:

"In the first place he was an exceedingly handsome young man and his clothes were the latest cut and quite outdid anything in the cowboy town. He was a real acquisition and everybody knew it. Mr. Aldrich remembered that he was a particularly graceful dancer and credited him with giving the town its first real social thrill."

People marveled at Sluss and his love of culture. He had a private library filled with works that included Shakespeare, Henry Ward Beecher and John Burroughs. A friend of his, Mrs. Charles Sharp, was quoted as saying in the Aug. 7, 1926, Wichita Eagle: "He was exceedingly proud of his library, which was one of the finest in the state. His selection of books reflected his literary tastes. He despised what was not of permanent value."

And though he refused to have stories written about him, local people considered him worthy of note.

The Eagle eulogized on Aug. 5, 1926: "No more shall his courtly manners teach us that propriety or demeanor which we, in these more hurried times, too often forget; hushed forever is the voice of his advocacy, a voice which never failed to bring assistance to the court."

William Wallace Hays

County sheriff valued his beard

When it came to his whiskers, William Wallace Hays put safety first.

His beard was so long that he would tuck it under his belt whenever he worked in his grain mills, for fear it would get caught in a gear.

So prized and well-known was

Hays' beard that an American Indian friend once wove a strip of red flannel into the whiskers as a decoration.

But Hays also is remembered for founding the town of Haysville and for serving as sheriff of Sedgwick County in the late 1880s. Hays shortened his beard when he

served as sheriff, Ellington said. "It was for the practical sake of appearance."

Hays and his family came to Sedgwick County from Illinois in 1871. He was accompanied by his parents, his wife, Julia, and five children. Together, they started a farm 12 miles south of Wichita.

William Hays, sheriff from 1886 to 1889, was known for his ability to reason with a crowd with a shotgun slung over his arm.

That first year, Hays built a sod house. The next, he hunted buffalo and hauled the hides back to Wichita at a profit. By 1874, the family's wheat and corn were planted and almost ready to be harvested when clouds of grasshoppers devoured the crops.

The loss prompted Hays to build a grist mill on Cowskin Creek, which ran through his farm. That same year he founded Haysville.

The family remained on the farm until 1885. Hays, however, went to Colorado in 1881. He stayed there for several years and ran a silver mine.

The Hays home was a big attraction for the surrounding area. Near the house was a 10-acre walnut grove where Fourth of July celebrations, picnics and other gatherings were held.

In 1885 Hays returned to Sedgwick County, moved to Wichita and ran for county sheriff.

He was elected in 1886 and was known for his ability to reason with a crowd with a shotgun slung over his arm. He was sheriff until 1889.

Local papers of the day indicate that he prided himself on being a staunch Republican. His first vote was cast for Abraham Lincoln.

Hays moved from the area at the turn of the century and joined the Alaska gold rush. He eventually moved to Tacoma, Wash., where he died in 1916. He was 76 years old.

Bat Masterson

Legendary lawman called Sedgwick County home

Bat Masterson and his brothers never tamed Wichita.

But the Mastersons did claim Sedgwick County as their home and maintained ties to the area into the 20th century.

It was a common thing for Bat to return to the scene of the family homestead and visit his parents and neighbors. He felt an allegiance to Sedgwick County.

The Masterson family came to Wichita from Illinois in 1870 and lived on an 80-acre farm near Sunnydale, 14 miles northeast of Wichita. Thomas and Catherine Masterson had seven children—five sons and two daughters. Three of the sons, Ed, William and Jim, became Old West legends.

Ed, the eldest, was born in 1852. William B. "Bat" was born in 1853. And Jim was born in 1855. During the fall of 1872, the three spent a great deal of time hunting buffalo on Kiowa Creek, which runs through Ford, Kiowa, Clark and Comanche counties.

Henry Raymond was a friend of the Masterson brothers and frequently hunted with them. Raymond recorded in his journal in January 1873 that he, Ed and Jim,

having sold their buffalo meat, started for Sedgwick County by wagon. To pass the time on the trip, the brothers shot at telegraph poles. The trip was uneventful except for a stop in Larned, where, Raymond wrote, "A fair senorita asked me to invest a note with her."

Back in Sedgwick County, Raymond's brother, Theodore, married a schoolteacher, Ida Curtis. The Wichita Eagle on April 30, 1874, reported that several Mastersons attended the wedding.

William Masterson was almost always referred to as Bat. Some Western historians have indicated that he earned his nickname by using a cane to subdue his opponents. But in his journal, Raymond says that Bat's middle name was Bartholomew, which was shortened to Bart and then to Bat.

All three brothers figured prominently as lawmen in Dodge City's cow town days. Ed was the city marshal until, at age 26, he was killed by a cowboy on April 9, 1878. At the time, Bat was sheriff of Ford County and Jim was a deputy sheriff. One year later, Jim was city marshal of Dodge City.

The papers recorded the inci-

Bat Masterson's nickname probably came from a shortening of his middle name, not from using a cane to subdue his opponents.

dents with the Mastersons from time to time.

Dodge City was tamed by the 1880s. By 1889, Jim Masterson had left for Oklahoma. He was one of the first settlers in Guthrie, served as a deputy sheriff of Logan County, and in 1893 became a deputy U.S.

marshal. He died on April 1, 1895, of consumption.

Bat remained Ford County sheriff until the November 1879 election, which he lost to Charles Roden. He checked in his sheriff's star and was reported to be a faro dealer in the Southwest. He eventually became a sportswriter for the Morning Telegraph in New York City.

He died in 1921 behind his desk at the Morning Telegraph. That same year, Thomas Masterson, the father of the famous Mastersons, died in Wichita.

Jack Ledford

His outlaw past finally caught up with him

John "Jack" Ledford was the type of man parents didn't want their daughters to marry.

A horse thief, murderer and robber, Ledford and his Star-Bar-Half-Moon Gang ruled the Arkansas River valley during Wichita's early days. Most local women and children feared him, with the exception of 16-year-old Alice Harris, stepdaughter of one of the town's most prominent families.

Ledford first met Harris in her stepfather's hotel, the Buckhorn Tavern. Henry Vigus had built the one-story log building, which was Wichita's first hotel, at what is now the northeast corner of Ninth and Waco. And in it, he had placed a music box.

Dances were held in the evenings. And one night when Ledford was there and the box stuck, he drew his revolver and shot it to pieces.

It was on that note that Harris and Ledford grew to love each other—much to the chagrin of Vigus.

Ledford was an Army scout during the Civil War under Gen. Phil Sheridan.

After the war, Ledford was stationed at Camp Beecher. Newspaper accounts indicate Ledford had some severance pay coming, but the Army quartermaster disagreed about the amount. And when his crony from the Civil War, Sheridan, asked for Ledford's services, his commanding officer wouldn't let him go.

The dissatisfied Ledford then stole a couple of Army mules and sold them to liquidate what he thought was part of his severance pay bill. A warrant was issued for

John "Jack" Ledford lived and died by the gun.

his arrest.

After that, Ledford seemed to lose interest in scouting for the government and turned outlaw.

For nearly two years, he made a living robbing stagecoaches and stealing horses. Finally, at age 27, he met Harris who, at 16, was one of the prettiest girls in town.

"One day the girl was standing in front of her father when Ledford came riding down Douglas Avenue like the wind," The Wichita Eagle reported. "He drew near the platform, but did not stop. As he reached the girl he swung partially from his saddle, caught her around the waist and raised her into the saddle. For half an hour they galloped about town, she sitting on the great Kentucky horse in front of her sweetheart, the picture of contentment and happiness."

When Ledford was later wounded in a stagecoach robbery

and thought to be dying, he sent for Harris. She came to his bedside, along with a Wichita doctor who had been kidnapped and blindfolded by members of Ledford's gang.

As Ledford healed, he asked Harris to marry him. She told him he would have to give up his outlaw ways. He agreed and on Dec. 22, 1870, the two applied for a marriage certificate.

To prove his love, Ledford bought a hotel, at what is now the northwest corner of Third and Main, and named it the Harris House.

Ledford ran for sheriff in the fall of 1870, promising, "If I am elected sheriff of this county there will be no more horses stolen around these parts." Ledford won but never served; the election was declared void because of too many irregularities.

Nevertheless, all was going well for the Ledfords until an old sweetheart of Harris', Sam Lee, showed up in Wichita. Lee noticed there was a $2,000 reward out for Jack Ledford and notified the officers at Fort Harker.

Military troops were called in, and on Feb. 28, 1871, they arrived in Wichita to arrest Ledford on charges of robbery and murder involving a government train and its teamsters. The troops surrounded the Harris House and searched the premises.

Ledford was across the street in George DeAmour's saloon. Sensing that something was wrong, he started for a back door that led to an outhouse.

He was unarmed, and a friend tossed him two old and rusty pistols. Ledford hid in the outhouse as the troops surrounded it.

Finally he opened the door and started shooting. He was shot once in the wrist and twice in the back, the last bullet entering his spine. He was carried back to the hotel and died an hour later.

He is buried in Highland Ceme-tery. His tombstone is government issued and reads: "K.J. Ledford, Co. K, Second Missouri Light Artillery."

Mike and John Meagher

Brothers in law enforcement kept the peace

During the rougher and row-dier moments of Wichita's cow town days, Mike and John Meagher offered some balancing law and order.

The brothers arrived in Sedgwick County in 1868 along with their father, Timothy, and mother, Ellen. The family came from Ireland and soon were well-thought-of residents of the young town.

Mike Meagher was appointed city marshal in April 1871 and held that position for five of the next six years. John Meagher at first was his assistant and was elected sheriff in the fall of 1871.

But it wasn't just the brothers who carried influence.

Ellen Meagher still is considered the "mother of Wichita's Catholic churches." Many of the city's early Masses were celebrated in the Meagher home before a church was built.

Of the two brothers, Mike Meagher seemed better suited for law enforcement. John Meagher served one term as sheriff and then traveled into Indian Territory, according to Joe Snell, past executive director of the Kansas State Historical Society and co-author of the book "Why the West Was Wild."

Mike Meagher was recognized as one of the more efficient lawmen in Kansas history.

"With nothing of the daredevil or reckless bravado in his composition, Mike Meagher did not know the meaning of personal fear," said an article in The Wichita Eagle on Dec. 22, 1881. "Many a times and oft has he faced death upon these streets with a bravery, fortitude and composure beyond the power of words to describe."

Mike Meagher, left, was city marshal of Wichita and brother John was sheriff. They left Wichita in 1879 and moved to Caldwell.

He did it with a look.

At least that's what the local papers at the time reported as one of his best qualities. He also ran his office efficiently. He did it by enforcing a city ordinance to check visitors' guns at the marshal's office on North Main.

While he was marshal, Mike Meagher killed one man. And that shooting of Sylvester Powell was what ultimately led to his own death four years later.

On Jan. 3, 1877, The Wichita Weekly Beacon reported the shooting:

"Meagher ran around by the New York store and as he turned the corner, he saw Powell approaching with his right hand in his pocket. Supposing that he meant to make an attack, Mike shot, the ball taking effect through or near the heart, causing almost instant death. As he fell, Powell exclaimed, 'My God, what have I done?' "

When the cattle trade shifted away from Wichita, the Meagher brothers left in 1879 and moved to Caldwell. There, in 1881, a cousin of Powell's, Jim Talbot, shot and killed Mike Meagher to avenge Powell's death.

Mike Meagher's body was returned to Wichita and buried in Maple Grove Cemetery. John Meagher moved to California and died in 1914.

"In my opinion, Mike Meagher was one of the finest officers that Wichita and Caldwell ever had," Snell said. "He has largely gone unsung. Nobody has ever written much on Mike Meagher. And that's a shame because he enforced the law with less violence than other lawmen.

"Maybe that was his problem, he didn't shoot more people."

Ellen Meagher still is known as the "mother of Wichita's Catholic Churches."

Wyatt Earp

Arrests were few during his Wichita days

Hollywood may have billed Wyatt Earp as the fast-shooting, peace-loving lawman who tamed the wild West, but his days in Wichita were largely uneventful.

In his one year as a Wichita police officer, Earp rounded up stray dogs and picked dead animals off the streets, arrested a few drunks, and was supposed to collect monthly fines from the city's prostitutes, one of whom was his sister-in-law.

"He didn't amount to a whole heck of a lot," said Joe Snell, past executive director of the Kansas State Historical Society.

"His career in Wichita was pretty lackluster."

In fact, local historians say, Earp was dismissed from his duties as a police officer after he brawled with a city marshal candidate and could not account for fines he collected from prostitutes.

Snell said that Earp, originally from Illinois, may have arrived in Wichita as early as May 1874. On April 21, 1875, he was appointed to the Wichita police force, under Marshal Mike Meagher.

Earp's first recorded Wichita arrest—of a horse thief wanted in Coffey County—was reported in The Weekly Beacon on May 12, 1875.

On Dec. 15, 1875, The Beacon again mentioned Earp:

"On last Wednesday, Policeman Erp (sic) found a stranger lying near the bridge in a drunken stupor. He took him to the 'cooler' and on searching him found in the neighborhood of $500 on his person. He may congratulate himself that his lines, while he was drunk, were cast in such a pleasant place as Wichita, as there are but few other places where that $500 roll would ever have been heard from. The integrity of our police force has never been seriously questioned."

The Jan. 12, 1876, issue of The Beacon said Earp was involved in a

Wyatt Earp was a Wichita police officer for about a year, beginning in 1875.

freak accident:

"Last Sunday night, while policeman Erp (sic) was sitting with two or three others in the back room of the Custom House saloon, his revolver slipped from his holster, and in falling to the floor, the hammer, which was resting on the cap, is supposed to have struck the chair, causing a discharge of one of the barrels. The ball passed through his coat, struck the north wall, then glanced off and passed out through the ceiling.

"It was a narrow escape and the occurrence got up a lively stampede from the room. One of the demoralized was under the impression that someone had fired through the window from the outside."

The Custom House Billiard Hall was operated by Charles Chattner and was at No. 14 Main Street—north of the alley that now separates One Main Place and the Kansas State Bank and Trust drive-through facility on Main.

Patrick Glynn, who portrays 1870s Sedgwick County Sheriff Henry Dunning for Old Cowtown Museum, has researched Wichita's early city records and newspapers. Glynn said Earp was employed as a police officer for only one year. Earp was dismissed by city officials after prostitution fines he was to

The Custom House Billiard Hall, which used to occupy this site on Main, was where Wyatt Earp nearly shot himself.

have collected were missing.

Glynn said the money police officers collected in gambling, liquor and prostitution fines was the only revenue for the city and county.

"There were no property taxes, no sales tax," Glynn said. "This was money made from cowboy money."

In addition to the missing money, Earp was involved in a fight with William Smith, a candidate for city marshal. He was arrested for violating peace and order, fined $30 and dismissed from the police force.

Not long after that, Earp left town and went to Dodge City. In 1881, he and his two brothers, Virgil and Morgan, and "Doc" Holliday shot it out with Ike Clanton's gang in the gunfight at the OK Corral in Tombstone, Ariz. Three members of Clanton's gang were killed; Earp's brothers were wounded.

It wasn't until 50 years later, in the biography "Wyatt Earp: Frontier Marshal" by Stuart Lake, that Earp's cowboy days were glamorized. Actor Hugh O'Brien elevated Earp to superstar status in the ABC-TV series that ran in the late 1950s and early 1960s.

But those stories were not always accurate. Some accounts portrayed Earp as a Wichita marshal when, in fact, he was only a police officer.

"Either Earp or Stuart Lake embellished the stories," Snell said. "I knew Stuart Lake, and he defended his biography even though there were some things in it that were not entirely accurate."

Earp ended up selling real estate in Los Angeles. He died Jan. 13, 1929, in bed, with his boots off. He was 81.

Catherine McCarty and Billy the Kid

Notorious gunslinger grew up on city streets

The wild West has been tamed at the southeast corner of 21st and Oliver, where Unity Church of Wichita now stands. But in 1870, it was the home of one of the West's most notorious outlaws.

Henry McCarty, later known as Billy the Kid, arrived in Wichita in the summer of 1870 with his mother, Catherine McCarty, and his younger brother, Joe. Henry was 11. And though his days as an outlaw were still to come, by the time his family left Wichita barely a year later, he and his mother both had developed reputations—he as a street urchin and she as a business leader.

The widow McCarty and her two sons arrived in Wichita from Indianapolis in July 1870, said the late Waldo Koop, a local historian and author of the book "Billy the Kid, the Trail of a Kansas Legend."

Koop said a business district was developing along what is now Main Street, north of Central, and McCarty purchased several lots in the area and opened City Laundry.

When a petition to incorporate Wichita was approved later that month, McCarty was the lone woman among the 124 signers.

But though she favored incorporating Wichita, McCarty moved her family out of town not long after the signing.

Koop said the little cow town may have been too raucous for her. Part of the problem, he said, was that Henry was exposed to numerous gunfights.

Early maps of the Wichita area indicate the family moved to the quarter section of land at what now is 21st and Oliver. Near it was a quarter section owned by William

Catherine McCarty moved with her sons to a quarter section where Unity Church of Wichita stands at 21st and Oliver.

When Henry McCarty became a teenager, he began his career as a gunfighter. Legend has it that he killed at least five men and as many as one "for every year of his age."

Antrim, who arrived in Wichita from Indianapolis at the same time as the McCartys.

McCarty and Antrim married on March 1, 1873, in New Mexico, Koop said.

But in 1870, Koop said, Antrim helped the McCartys establish a home as they erected a cabin, dug a well and storm cellar, and planted hedges and fruit trees. And he taught Henry to work the land.

Plans for the homestead were cut short in the spring of 1871, when Antrim and the McCartys began selling their property.

"It's not difficult to reconstruct the reason, for one can imagine the signs of ill health for the widow, a trip to a physician and the dread pronouncement of tuberculosis," Koop wrote in his book. "Not an uncommon affliction in those times, its diagnosis was generally followed by a recommendation for a move to the high and dry climates of Colorado and New Mexico."

McCarty died less than a decade later in Silver City, N.M., Koop said.

When Henry became a teenager, he began his career as a gunfighter. Legend has it that he killed at least five men and as many as one "for every year of his age." In 1881, when he was 22, Billy the Kid was shot by Pat Garrett in Fort Sumner, N.M.

The news of his death spread throughout the nation. In Wichita, Marshall Murdock, editor of The Wichita Eagle, wrote this epitaph: "Billy the Kid, an account of whose tragic death we published two weeks since, formerly lived in Wichita, and many of the early settlers remember him as a street gamin in the days of longhorns."

Rowdy Joe Lowe

He put the bite in Delano's raucous reputation

Metropolitan Baptist Church sits serenely today at the corner of Douglas and McLean, its steeple towering over the rush of downtown traffic.

But during the 1870s, the site of the church was anything but serene. Along a 2½-block stretch of Douglas just west of the Arkansas River stood the rip-roaring town of Delano. Prostitutes, cowboys and gunfighters walked the streets, and Wichita townspeople complained that the town had no law and order.

And though Delano lasted less than a decade, the town in its heyday was considered scandalous by its neighbors to the east.

In 1872, for instance, The Wichita Eagle reported that dance hall girls from Delano were seen bathing in the river "with nothing on except the moles on their backs," said the late Waldo Koop.

The town sprang up in the early 1870s as a "pop-off valve." The town offered options to the cowboy, who, after long cattle drives, craved a chance to drink, dance and socialize with "ladies of the evening."

Named after Columbus Delano, secretary of the interior under President Ulysses Grant, the town had no local police and no law requiring that guns be checked.

Some of Delano's more notorious residents were dance hall proprietor "Rowdy Joe" Lowe and his business rival, Edwin T. Beard, also known as "Red Beard" because of his enormous red mustache.

Delano, to the right in this non-scale drawing, was a place for cowboys to blow off steam. The town was named for Columbus Delano.

"Rowdy Joe" Lowe ran a saloon in Delano. He once bit off a man's nose.

By the time he came to Wichita, Lowe had a reputation as a man without scruples. Lowe had earned his nickname in Denver, Koop learned, where he was involved in a saloon fight. When a local lawman demanded that the combatants apologize, Lowe is reported to have told his adversary, "Come here. I want to kiss and make up." Then he seized the man and bit off the end of his nose, Koop said.

Lowe and his wife, "Rowdy Kate," came to Wichita in 1870. He was in Wichita long enough to steal a mule and win an acquittal when the only witness against him failed to appear in court. He left Wichita after that, but returned in 1872 to run a dance hall in Delano, Koop said.

On July 26 of that year, The Eagle reported: "A fracas occurred at the dance house of Joseph Lowe on last Friday evening, in which a man by the name of Joseph Walters, who was at the time drunk, was badly bruised and cut about the face and head by a revolver in the hands of the keeper of the house. At this writing, the wounded man lies in a very critical condition."

Not long after, Rowdy Joe became involved in a feud with Red Beard because of competition over drinking and dancing customers.

It culminated in a shoot-out. The Eagle, on Oct. 30, 1873, reported that both men were drunk at the time of the shooting.

It's quiet now, with businesses and a church, but the area near Douglas and McLean used to be wild.

"Rowdy Joe was shot in the back of the neck with a pistol ball. The wound is not dangerous. Red was wounded in the arm and hip by buckshot from a shotgun. The chances are that he will lose the lower part of his arm. A poor dance girl, Annie Franklin, received a shot in the abdomen, which the doctors think must prove fatal. Bill Anderson was shot in the head, was alive at last accounts. Rowdy Joe gave himself up and is now out on $2,000 bail."

Red Beard died about three weeks later from infection in his wounds. He is buried in Highland Cemetery.

Rowdy Joe Lowe left Wichita in 1873. In 1899, The Eagle reported that he had been killed in a Denver saloon. Lowe, 72, had insulted the Denver Police Department and was shot by a former policeman.

Delano lasted only seven years after Lowe left town. It had a post office that opened on April 5, 1871, and closed on Jan. 14, 1876. Local records show that the post office was temporarily reopened on April 7, 1879, but was phased out when Delano was incorporated into Wichita in December 1880.

Ellington said the need for the town ended in 1876 when Texas cattle herds no longer came to Wichita because of quarantine laws stemming from Texas cattle fever.

Prostitutes, Prohibitionists and Populists

Rea Woodman

She made history her story

Rea Woodman knew how to tell a story.

In verse or plays, essays or the classroom, Woodman was, for a time, Wichita's leading historian.

By right, she had her roots there.

Born on Feb. 10, 1870, in Jacksonville, Ill., Woodman was barely 9 months old when she and her family came to Wichita. No housing was available, so the family spent the winter in Emporia. In the spring of 1871, they returned to Wichita, where Woodman's father, William, opened a general store on North Main. Because farmers needed credit, he also opened the First Arkansas Valley Bank.

When she was 3, Rea Woodman was kidnapped by Arapaho Indians. Her father, W.C. "Buffalo Bill" Mathewson and N.A. English rode off to rescue her and soon caught up with the Indians.

A biographical sketch on Woodman says her father and Mathewson pretended that they did not know who she was:

"They acted like it was just a friendly visit, without even mentioning the child. But the Indians were anxious to sell the white child, so they began telling about this white child that they had. Mr. Woodman didn't even act interested but finally agreed to see the child. He remarked that he had several better-looking children at home, plus she was quite dirty. The Indians became worried that the white men wouldn't trade for the child, so Rea was ransomed for fifty cents and a pocket knife."

Back with her family, Woodman

Rea Woodman was kidnapped by Indians when she was 3 years old.

grew up at 901 N. Waco. The home originally served as Wichita's first hotel, the Munger House, and is now at Old Cowtown Museum.

While in Wichita, she attended Garfield University, now Friends University. She received her bachelor's degree from Drake University in 1891 and her master's from the University of Kansas in 1902. She did further graduate work at the University of Nebraska and the University of Minnesota.

English language and literature were her main interests, and she taught classes in them at Garfield, Drake and Nebraska.

She also wrote more than 30 plays for schools and colleges plus a series of 200 sketches on social

life in Wichita from 1880 to 1897. Those sketches were later compiled in a book, "Wichitana," published in 1948 and dedicated to Mathewson.

Woodman also wrote books of prose and poetry that included "The Noahs Afloat," "The Heart and the Crown," "Tumbleweed," "The Open Road," "In Memoriam" and "The Bobbie Bennett Plays for Children."

On May 18, 1951, The Wichita Eagle reported that "although Miss Woodman gained considerable recognition through her career, most of her many friends were won through her unusual personality. She was known as a person with a keen sense of humor, who could see a bright side to any situation. The advance of years did not dull this cheerful disposition."

For a time, Woodman lived on the East Coast. She was a tutor for Vassar College and did editorial work for the Neale Publishing Co. in New York. After living more than 30 years away from her hometown, in 1927 Woodman moved back to Wichita and became part of the editorial staff of The Eagle.

She spent the remainder of her life writing and conducting private classes in English, philosophy and creative writing.

Woodman died on May 12, 1951. She was 81 and called by some of the state's leading newspapers "Kansas' most colorful pioneer." In 1962, an elementary school at 2500 Hiram was named after her.

Ellington said, "She really brought out the human interest of our history."

Mary Elizabeth Lease

Hypatia Club founder challenged the times

Members of Women of Hypatia admit that they no longer raise eyebrows or

spark headlines in city papers the way their founder did 100 years ago.

But Mary Elizabeth Lease had little trouble doing either with her ad in the Jan. 21, 1886, Wichita Eagle.

Mary Elizabeth Lease caused a ruckus by inviting women to join Hypatia, which meets today at 1215 N. Broadway.

It read, "We would most earnestly invite the intelligent women of Wichita, the artists, musicians, teachers, actors, lecturers, and all women having the advancement of their sex in view, to meet Saturday, Jan. 23, at 3 o'clock at the residence of Mrs. Harry Hill, 321 Topeka Avenue."

It caused such turmoil in the community that The Eagle's editor, Marshall Murdock, wrote an editorial urging husbands to keep their wives at home, said Carol Rutledge, a former Wichita resident and author of "The Women of Hypatia, 1886-1986."

Nevertheless, nine women did band together to form a social club. They named themselves after Hypatia—a fifth-century Greek female philosopher and educator. And their intent was to promote the cultural and intellectual interests of women.

During the early years, members met in their homes. In October 1934, they bought a house at 1215 N. Broadway and have been using it ever since. The Hypatia Club house became a local historic landmark in 1980 and was placed on the National Register of Historic Places in 1991.

The club's 200 members say they belong to the oldest women's club in the state. Hypatia still follows a social club format. Programs reflect intellectual and cultural interests.

Born in 1853 in New York, Mary Elizabeth Clymen came to Kansas when she was 15 to teach at the Osage Mission. She married Charles Lease, a druggist, and by 1883, they had four children and were living in Wichita.

Not long after the Hypatia controversy, Lease also became a forceful spokeswoman for the Populist Party. As her notoriety grew, Republican newspapers attacked her.

The Wellington Monitor called her "a miserable character of womanhood and hideously ugly of features and foul of tongue."

In Raleigh, N.C., the newspaper likened Lease to John Brown, saying she invaded the South "with the declaration that the Negro should be made the equal of the white man and that all differences between the sexes should be obliterated. Great God, what next from Kansas?"

Rutledge said Lease finally turned her back on the Populist Party when it would not support women's right to vote.

In 1897, Rutledge said, with a failed marriage and the mortgage due on her home at 330 N. Wabash, Lease sold her house and moved to New York City.

She never returned.

In 1933, when she was 80, Lease told a reporter that her biggest disappointment in life was the realization that she would never become president of the United States.

She died later that year.

The legacy of Lease, though, isn't dwelt on by the members.

"We're glad she did those things, but it's like asking how much Lincoln is remembered today," said member Maybelle Bales. "Do we think about him every day? Like him, she was an event in history."

In 1934, the Women of Hypatia bought a house for their meetings. The Hypatia Club house won local landmark status in 1980 and still is used for meetings.

Jessie Clark

She brought music to Wichita's classrooms

I t used to be that whenever there was music in Wichita, Jessie Clark was not far behind.

Clark, a pioneer music teacher, was an institution for many of Wichita's early public school children, even though she almost lost her job after her first year of teaching.

Her contribution to Wichita was in inspiring young people to the field of music. Her approach wasn't with a stern lecture but with a subtle flair of humor.

Clark was born near Troy, N.Y., on Nov. 2, 1863. Her mother died when Clark was 11 years old, and her father placed her in a foster home. In 1882, she graduated from Robinson Female Seminary and taught English and composition at the Kingston Academy in New York for several years.

Then, in 1887, she came West, sending resumes to several cities. Wichita responded, and Clark was named music supervisor for all Wichita schools. Her salary was $50 a month.

The Wichita Eagle on April 10, 1955, in a story about the dedication of a new organ named in Clark's honor at East High School, described her by saying, "She charmed by brusqueness plus clowning and comical grimacing at off-pitch singing; by relentless demands towards perfection, plus merry eyes and an engulfing smile and by the mother-like love and

Jessie Clark endeared herself to the children through her dog, Piccolo, and her horse, Patsy.

nurture she gave in bounty to each child."

A lifelong friend, Edith Marshall, wrote at the time of Clark's death that Clark almost left Wichita after her first year.

"In the spring of 1888, Supt. Chidester did not recommend Miss Clark for reappointment," Marshall wrote. "He said he would commend her for any position from primary to High School—outside of Wichita, but he didn't like her personality and didn't want her in the schools. Behind a somewhat brusque exterior, Jessie Clark shielded as sensitive a soul as ever

assumed mortal form. She was hurt to the quick and would have started for New York the next day had I not interfered."

Nevertheless, Clark was reappointed and endeared herself to the children through her dog, Piccolo, and her horse, Patsy. Old newspaper accounts indicate that boys would fight in the school yard for a chance to assist Clark in carrying her books and to tend Patsy.

Clark was music supervisor for grade and high schools until 1914. By then, her territory had become so large, she asked to teach only high school classes. She taught orchestra, band and glee club as well as classes in history and harmony of music.

She organized mandolin and guitar clubs and soon added violins, cello and bass viols.

The Eagle reported that before the curtain rose on school performances, Clark would tap her music rack with her baton and whisper to the school choir loud enough to be heard:

"You're the most beautiful thing on Earth. Like paradise, just to look at you. I'm expecting you to sing just as well as you look."

Clark died on June 28, 1925. An organ in the East High School auditorium was purchased as a memorial to her.

She was one who against all obstacles decided to stay with her career.

Myra Warren McHenry

She crusaded for temperance, to her husband's chagrin

M yra Warren McHenry specialized in militant behavior.

Jailed at least 20 times, the hatchet-toting McHenry spent more than 50 years crusading

against whiskey, tobacco, rising skirt lines, high-heel shoes, and politicians and preachers whom she deemed hypocrites.

Once she said, "A Republican is a man who takes a drink of whiskey

and says he is dry; a Democrat is a man who drinks whiskey and does not lie out of it."

McHenry was Carry A. Nation's right-hand woman in Wichita. She held almost daily talks from the

"I like Wichita because there's so much corruption that it keeps me busy," Myra Warren McHenry once told reporters.

post office steps at Market and William and from the Sedgwick County Courthouse at Central and Main.

For most of Wichita's residents, she was a curiosity more than an effective warrior. Still, she became a legendary character in Wichita.

Myra Warren was born in Lafayette County, Mo., on March 28, 1848. Her mother was a niece of Jefferson Davis, president of the Confederacy. On March 28, 1872,

Warren married an attorney, J.A. McHenry, and they lived in the Wichita area.

She became interested in the temperance movement and fought to get Prohibition passed in Kansas—much to the embarrassment of her husband. Often she would publicly denounce his friends.

At one point, there was a warrant filed, charging her with insanity. She escaped, wearing men's clothing, and fled to Wichita. Her husband tried to divorce her, but she refused, saying marriages were made in heaven.

Nevertheless, the two were divorced.

In Wichita, she became an ardent supporter of Nation and a crusader against liquor and local politics. She carried a hatchet and smashed bottles of liquor. She spoke daily on the streets of Wichita, delivering speeches that were often two hours long. In 1908, a calendar hanging in an elevator at City Hall showing a woman with a low neckline so offended her that she bought some lace and stitched a collar to the calendar.

"I like Wichita because there's so much corruption that it keeps me busy," she told reporters.

In 1926, she publicly denounced

the secretary of the city manager and said things that the newspapers said were not fit to print. The secretary slapped McHenry and there was a lawsuit. The Wichita Beacon praised the secretary for the slapping.

"The Beacon has never advocated the policy of anyone taking the law into his own hands," the June 18, 1926, editorial read. "Nevertheless, the experience of this community with this vicious-minded old woman is such as would seem to justify to some extent the natural reaction of people whom she has slandered. She has been a nuisance and a disgrace which few well-organized communities would endure."

McHenry continued her crusades until an afternoon in June 1939. She slipped on steps as she made her daily trip to the Sedgwick County Courthouse, fell and went into a coma.

Two weeks later, she died at age 91.

"They ask me how an old lady like me has the grit and backbone to do the things I do," McHenry once said. "But when I die I hope this is not what they remember most about me. I want it known that my life has proved the word of God true."

Lucetta Fassett Carter

She never met a magazine she couldn't sell

Lucetta Fassett Carter's size didn't hamper her when it came to salesmanship.

Just after the turn of the century, the tiny Wichita woman held one company's record for selling the greatest number of magazines in one person's lifetime. She won contests. And she gave almost all her money to charity. She made substantial donations to the Wichita Children's Home, the Fairmount University library and the YWCA library.

She was personable and well-liked, selling The Saturday Evening Post for a living.

In a bibliophile paper, Hal Ross writes that she was born in Enosburgh Falls, Vt., on July 11, 1828. Lucetta Fassett was 16 when her father died and she went to work in a cloth factory. Four years later, in 1848, she married Nathaniel Carter. They had two children, George and Edward. Nathaniel died in 1868, and Carter took her children to Illinois. She lived there until 1880, when she moved to Wichita.

In 1885, Carter was living on a $750-a-year inheritance left by her late husband. It was then she read "What One Woman Can Do," a book that changed her life. She de-

cided to sell books to supplement her income.

She started her selling career in Winfield, where a local minister told her that she need not try, because 12 book agents had been in town the week before and none had been successful. Carter didn't leave until she had taken orders for 437 books and delivered 330 of them at $3 and $5 apiece.

Encouraged by her success, she signed a contract for $10,000 to sell the book "Through the Dark Continent," a travelogue of Africa. But people didn't buy, and she was left with an $8,000 debt to repay, which she did.

She established an office at the southeast corner of Topeka and Douglas. From there, she sold magazines and sets of Encyclopaedia Britannica. As her debt was repaid, she became a powerhouse on salesmanship. Her approach was simple: She would see people she knew on Wichita's streets and tell them, "I have signed you up for The Saturday Evening Post this year." Her customers were then expected to pay.

When couples were married, she gave subscriptions to The Saturday Evening Post to the husbands and the Ladies Home Journal to the wives. As the subscriptions ran out, she expected the couples to renew.

Curtis Publications gave her $1,000 for being its best salesman in the world—she sold the most subscriptions in the shortest amount of time. And she gave the money to the Wichita Children's Home. She furnished the first room in the Holyoke Cottage dormitory

Lucetta Fassett Carter was penniless when she died in 1919.

at Fairmount College. And when a neighbor left Carter $3,000, she added $2,000 of her own money and gave the $5,000 to build a parsonage for the Unitarian church.

She built water fountains throughout the city for people and

horses and donated thousands of dollars to local libraries.

In 1916, Carter suffered heat prostration and spent the next three years in Wesley Hospital, never fully recovering. At the time of her death, on July 4, 1919, she was penniless. That day, she had signed a check to a local maternity home, giving away the last penny she had.

"I tell you I am strapped," she is reported to have said. "I can't even afford to be cremated as I would like. . . . Maybe I can have a sundial at the foot of my grave and be buried at sunset between my boys."

Her funeral services were held before sunset, but she was buried between her sons, in Maple Grove Cemetery. There is no sundial on her grave, but there is an inscription:

"A noble woman, God's greatest gift to man. She devoted her life to the uplift of humanity. Love and Duty, her only creed."

Dixie Lee

There was a method to this madam—loyalty

Inez Oppenheimer wasn't just any "soiled dove."

As frontier prostitutes go, she was Wichita's last great madam, a flashy fixture of the community who was loyal to some of the city's most—and least—respected men.

The upstanding women of Wichita couldn't have cared less about Oppenheimer's loyalty.

"The respectable ladies always wanted to get rid of her," said Wilma Sehnert, an amateur historian who has researched Wichita's early years. "She was supposed to have been on the other side of the river . . . but she wouldn't go. She stayed in Wichita."

Little is known about Oppenheimer's background. She chose the professional name Dixie Lee partly as an advertising gimmick. Many of her customers were former Confederate sympathizers.

Dixie Lee became a well-known figure in Wichita's red-light district in the late 1800s. She ran three brothels at First and Wichita, near where the Garvey Center is today.

What was most exasperating to Wichitans of the time was that Dixie Lee was only one of a number of prostitutes in the city.

Joe Snell, past director of the Kansas State Historical Society and author of "Calico Queens and Painted Ladies," said that in 1874, Wichita had a population of 2,003. During the winter of 1873-1874, the town was visited by five to seven prostitutes a month. But the number rose to 50 in June, July and August when Texas cowboys drove their herds through town.

Although state laws made prostitution and brothel-keeping illegal, with fines of as much as $1,000 and county jail sentences of as much as

six months, officials in most Kansas towns chose to ignore the laws. Instead, they collected monthly "fines" as operating licenses.

The Wichita Eagle on May 28, 1874, reported that the fines paid by prostitutes and saloon owners brought in thousands of dollars. In Wichita, the prostitutes were fined $10 and madams $20.

Snell said that cowboys would come to town, "marry" a prostitute for a week, and take her to breakfast and dinner.

The women would issue tokens, known as brass checks, to the cowboys, encouraging them to come back. A typical house of the time, The China Doll in Dodge City, even posted prices, ranging from 10 cents to 50 cents, on its tokens.

Among the prostitutes, Dixie Lee was known for her flamboyant personality.

The Missouri-Pacific Railroad passenger station was the pride of Wichita in the early 1900s. In the right background is the roof of the Dixie Lee mansion.

"She was a good-natured old lady," Sehnert said. "She was spunky."

The Wichita Beacon reported that Dixie Lee's brothels were considered the most elegant in town and that she was loyal to the men on whom she lavished attention.

Dixie Lee wore diamonds. She was a small, good-looking brunette who was tastefully dressed in public. And she was known to display her wealth by driving an elegant carriage with matched, pure white horses on Sundays. Her passengers were her "girls."

In 1877, W.E. Stanley, then the Sedgwick County attorney, wrote to the Wichita City Council urging regulation of the brothels.

"Houses of prostitution are advertising themselves by open doors on some of the most public streets of our city, prostitutes in half-nude forms take their morning airings under the eyes of many of our most respectable citizens and flaunt the indicia of their trade in all public places and gatherings without hindrance from the authorities."

By the turn of the century, Stanley had changed his tune. Dixie Lee's brothels were situated on valuable downtown property that was coveted by city officials. In 1900, officials unsuccessfully attempted to close Wichita Street, where Dixie Lee's brothels were, to construct the Missouri-Pacific Railroad terminal. Stanley's law firm came to her defense. Stanley, however, did not want the publicity of defending Dixie Lee and kept a low profile.

Dixie Lee died in 1901, leaving an estate valued at $200,000. After a lengthy search for heirs, her father—a Methodist minister in a small Missouri town—was finally located. It was reported that he was shocked when he learned the nature of his daughter's profession, but accepted the money anyway.

Carry A. Nation

An enemy of drink, she began her crusade in a Wichita bar

Carry A. Nation had some nerve. The Medicine Lodge woman who opposed liquor and tobacco first made national news on Dec. 27, 1900, when she marched into Wichita's Hotel Carey, what is now the Eaton Hotel at the southwest corner of St. Francis and Douglas, and wrecked the bar.

Using a billiard ball and short pieces of iron attached to a cane, she broke the massive mirror behind the bar and smashed glasses and bottles. Then she hurled two rocks at the pride of the saloon—a life-size painting of "Cleopatra at the Roman Bath."

One of the rocks missed the target. The other broke the protective glass cover, but the painting was unharmed.

Nation was arrested and placed in the old Sedgwick County Jail. She was to have been released on bond, but a smallpox quarantine extended her stay to 20 days.

Wichita Eagle newsman Dave Leahy gave the story to the wire services and advised Nation that a hatchet would be a more colorful weapon to use against the bars.

She took his advice, and a crusade was born.

After Wichita, Nation's saloon-smashing mission included trips to Topeka and Kiowa. Eventually, she went on a public-speaking circuit, with stops in New York and England.

Born in Garrad County, Ky., in 1846, Nation and her family lived on several plantations in Kentucky before moving to Missouri in 1855.

Ten years later, she married a Civil War surgeon, Charles Lloyd, who was an alcoholic. Their life was hard, and when the finances depleted, Nation left Lloyd and returned to Missouri.

In an article called "Hatchet Hall," Nation said she then prayed

The bar at Wichita's Hotel Carey, now the Eaton Hotel, was badly damaged by Carry A. Nation on Dec. 27, 1900.

for a righteous, upstanding man to marry. That's when she met David Nation, a newspaper editor and minister who didn't drink or use tobacco in any form.

The couple moved to Medicine Lodge in 1890. In 1900, Nation began her campaign to rid the nation of alcohol and tobacco.

Nation was, in a sense, a publicity seeker. Her first name was originally spelled Carrie, but she changed it to Carry A. Nation.

When she took to the lecture circuit, she wore a little black bonnet, dressed in black alpaca and carried a big purse. In the purse were small hatchets, which she sold.

Nation died June 2, 1911, in Leavenworth. Followers of the Women's Christian Temperance Union gave the city of Wichita a memorial to Nation in 1918. It sat in front of the Union Station site

Carry A. Nation prays while locked up in the Sedgwick County Jail.

until Oct. 11, 1945, when a beer truck backed into the memorial and knocked it from its pedestal. The memorial still stands but is in Naftzger Park across from the Eaton Hotel.

Hattie Waller

Mystery girl still captures city's imagination

For more than 100 years, Hattie Waller—with a mysterious bouquet of flowers in her hand—and her dog have braved the elements.

Even now, the marble statue captures the interest and imagination of Wichitans as she gazes out over the city from her hill at Maple Grove Cemetery.

"She's always holding flowers," said Eric Cale, the cemetery's manager. "She has no known relatives here."

Hattie Waller was born Sept. 21, 1885, the only daughter of Fred and Clara Waller.

Fred Waller worked in banking, first as a teller for Wichita National Bank and then as a cashier for the Fourth National Bank, said Beverly Henline, a local history researcher. His wife, Clara Furlong Waller, came from a prominent Wichita family.

The couple lived at 426 N. Emporia, and their home "was the scene of much social gaiety for they were cordial and hospitable and enjoyed great popularity," according to an article in the Nov. 18, 1928, Wichita Eagle.

At the time of her death, on April 30, 1889, Hattie Waller was 4½ years old. Cemetery records list the cause of death as "azdeocephalus." A newspaper article said the cause of death was similar to typhoid fever.

Hattie's parents hired Stephen Hesse, the German stonecutter who did the work on the Old City Hall building, to erect a monument to her. Hesse selected some photographs of Hattie and her dog and used those as models while he worked on a block of Vermont marble.

The Eagle reported in 1928: "The long skirt which reached her ankles was very full and fashioned of an elaborate pattern of solid embroidery. All of these difficult and intricate details have been reproduced in stone with amazing fidel-

Mike Hutmacher/The Wichita Eagle

A statue of Hattie Waller and her dog commemorates the girl's grave in Maple Grove Cemetery. When she died in 1889, Hattie was 4½ years old.

ity. The expression of her face and the grace of her pose have been caught by the sculptor with a skill that makes the little image strikingly lifelike. The water spaniel at her feet with his thick, curly coat, must have looked in life much the same as we see him today in stone."

Cale said Hattie's grave was originally in Highland Cemetery but was moved across Hillside to Maple Grove in 1892 because "it was more prestigious then to be buried in Maple Grove." The Waller family left Wichita a few years later and moved to the East Coast.

Hattie's grave is just within the Hillside boundary of Maple Grove about midway between the north entrance and the Ninth Street entrance.

Lorene Kerns, a 78-year-old grandmother, is one person who cares about the little girl and her dog.

"I was born in 1912, and the Maple Grove Cemetery was our playground growing up," Kerns said. "I was always fascinated with that little girl. I always wondered if the dog was buried with her."

Kerns said the grave never had flowers on it until she started putting them there about a decade ago. That's when she learned from an article that the girl had no relatives in Wichita. Kerns began placing artificial flowers in the girl's arms, varying the bouquet according to the season.

"I wire them on so that they stay," she said. "I drive by there quite a bit, so I notice if the wind has happened to blow them down. It doesn't happen that often, and when it does, I just replace them."

Kerns said all of her relatives are buried in Maple Grove Cemetery, and that's where she will be buried. She has asked her 13-year-old granddaughter, Beth Caruso, to care for Hattie Waller and her dog when she's dead.

"She will keep the tradition up for me," Kerns says.

Chief Satanta, Indian Tunes and a Bowl of Chili

"The aim of the school . . . is to train Indian boys for leadership of their own people. This comes from the realization that the Indian must make his own way in a short time. If he is not trained for that time, he may suffer extermination."
—Henry Roe Cloud, founder of the Roe Institute, later renamed the American Indian Institute

Satanta

Kiowa chief knew when to blow his horn

A boulder surrounded by houses and a dog-training school mark the spot where more than 3,000 Indians, scouts and military men gathered in the fall of 1865 to outline the Little River Peace Treaty.

Although peace from the treaty was short-lived, the conference served three functions: It was a step in making Kansas safe for settlers; it allowed government officials to express concern over the Sand Creek Massacre, which happened the previous year; and it drew together some of the most powerful leaders of Indian nations. Among them was Kiowa Chief Satanta, who was notorious for his strategic raids against the U.S. military and white settlements.

He was highly respected by both the white and Indian people. Satanta was a staunch, stern individual with piercing eyes and a determined look. He took his mission seriously and longed for peace.

When Satanta came to the fork of the Arkansas and Little Arkansas

Kiowa Chief Satanta caused confusion by blowing his brass French horn during a battle with Kit Carson's troops.

rivers, his name was already well-known among Indian tribes and government officials. In the book "Indian Chiefs," by Russell Freed-

man, there is a story dating back to 1864. That's when a government physician visited the southern plains to vaccinate Indians against smallpox and stayed in Satanta's village for four days. He reported that Satanta "is a fine-looking Indian, very energetic and sharp as a briar. He puts on a great deal of style, spreads a carpet for his guests to sit on. . . . He has a brass French horn, which he blew vigorously when the meals were ready."

A few months after the visit, the Army dispatched 350 volunteer troops commanded by Kit Carson to seek revenge on the Kiowas for raids against white settlers. It was reported that 1,000 Kiowa and Comanche warriors fought the troops and that, as the soldiers retreated, there was widespread confusion because a bugler kept sounding advance.

It was Satanta blowing his own horn.

The 1865 peace council, on what is now the northwest corner of Seneca and 61st North, began with an apology by the chairman of the commission, J.B. Sanborn, for the Sand Creek Massacre. The massacre occurred when Colorado militia attacked a group of Cheyenne Indians near Fort Lyon, Colo., killing 450 men, women and children. The treaty commissioners proposed compensating the Indians financially and told them that most Americans did not approve of the attack.

The treaty required the tribes to stay away from roads, trails, settlers and military outposts, and to agree to leave their hunting ranges for marked reservations in Indian Territory, now Oklahoma. In compensation, the Kiowa and Comanche Indians were to receive $15 for each tribe member and limited hunting rights.

The peace was short-lived; two years later, the U.S. government called a second meeting at Medicine Lodge.

Laura Rauch/The Wichita Eagle

A plaque attached to a boulder at the northwest corner of Seneca and 61st North marks the spot where Indians, scouts and military men signed the Little River Peace Treaty.

At the first meeting, journalists called Satanta "the Orator of the Plains."

"All the land south of the Arkansas River belongs to the Kiowas and the Comanches, and I don't want to give any of it away. I love the land and the buffalo and will not part with it," Satanta said.

"A long time ago, this land belonged to our fathers, but when I go up the river, I see camps of soldiers on its banks. These soldiers cut down my timber. They kill my buffalo. And when I see that, I feel as though my heart will burst with sorrow."

Through the years, there were several skirmishes between the Indians and settlers, with Satanta sometimes held accountable. Wichita newspapers reported that a Pat Hennesey—a Wichita man who hauled wagons—was said to have lost his scalp to Satanta after traveling into Indian Territory on a freight consignment from Wichita to the Anadarko Agency.

In 1874, Satanta was imprisoned by the U.S. government to serve a life sentence in the Texas State Prison. In August 1878, the prison superintendent reported that Satanta was in declining health and feeble and urged that he be released.

The request was denied.

On Sept. 11, 1878, Satanta threw himself headfirst from a second-story hospital balcony and died a few hours later. He was 58.

The Wichita Indians

They struggled to survive on the banks of the Little Arkansas

The Wichita Indians, brought to the area through a government relocation project, arrived on the eastern banks of the Little Arkansas River in the spring of 1864.

The 1,500 Wichitas and members of affiliated tribes spent that winter along the river in the area between what is now Murdock and 13th Street. They were hungry, and they had no clothes, guns or horses.

But even though they were removed from their original site, many believed this land was their home. It was where their ancestors used to roam and settle.

By the beginning of the 18th century, the Wichitas, descendants of the Quivira Indians, had been

Mead Island, seen from Minisa Bridge on 13th Street, was the northern edge of the area settled by the Wichita Indians between 1864 and 1867.

driven by the Osage and Comanches to what is now northern Texas. At the start of the Civil War, the Wichitas were moved to southwestern Oklahoma because of their sympathy toward the North.

They were removed for their safety and placed under the supervision of Jesse Chisholm, a half-breed Cherokee.

But as tensions among Indians increased, the U.S. government moved the Wichitas from Fort Cobb, near what is Lawton, Okla. The Indians wandered for the next few years until they settled at the Little Arkansas River, said Avis German, who once researched the history of the Wichita Indians for a Wichita State University master's

thesis.

That first season along the Little Arkansas, the Wichitas managed to kill enough buffalo to survive. Then the predominantly agricultural people planted crops and built lodges.

The name Wichita means "painted faces" or "scattered lodges."

The Wichitas arrived in Kansas in the fall of 1862, near Belmont in Woodson County. Because the land along the Little Arkansas was owned by the Osage Indians, the Wichitas waited in Woodson County until permission could be obtained for them to move to the present site of Wichita.

After they moved to the banks of

In 1927, Wichita Indians from Anadarko, Okla., built a grass lodge on Mead Island as a sign of good will.

the Little Arkansas River, they stayed about 3 ½ years.

"It was a very sad and detrimental experience for them," German said.

By late fall of 1867, Elias Durfee had established a trading post, which was the catalyst for attracting settlers to the Wichita area. Military troops who passed through brought cholera. The Indians had no immunity to the disease, and many of them died.

When tensions had eased again after the Civil War, the Wichitas were ordered to relocate again, and some asked permission to stay in the area long enough to harvest their crops.

On Oct. 27, 1867, the Wichitas left on a 260-mile walk to the Washita River, near Anadarko, Okla., where they had been assigned by the government to live.

In 1868, J.R. Mead, one of Wichita's developers, suggested that the new town springing up around the trading post on the Little Arkansas be called Wichita.

German said Mead helped the Indians in many ways. "During the time they were here, they hunted buffalo and raised gardens. When they left, they left their grass-covered lodges and garden plots."

In 1924, through a Wichita Booster Club project, some Wichita residents went to Anadarko. The Indians offered to build a lodge in Wichita as an expression of good will. In 1927, a grass lodge was constructed on Mead Island near 13th Street. The lodge was destroyed in the late 1940s when two boys playing there built a fire that got out of control.

Henry Roe Cloud

To him, formal education was an Indian birthright

Henry Roe Cloud spent most of his lifetime as a superachiever.

He was a graduate of Yale, was listed in Who's Who of America and became one of the nation's leading reformers for the rights of American Indians.

One of his first efforts at reform started in Wichita in 1915 with the founding of the Roe Institute, later renamed the American Indian Institute. At the time, it was one of three all-Indian high schools in the United States.

"He was a well-educated man who was a full-blooded Winnebago," said John Washee, a Cheyenne-Arapaho who lives in Wichita and who attended the school from 1926 to 1928. "He wanted to educate young Indians just like he was."

Cloud was born in Nebraska in 1884. He was adopted by missionaries Walter and Mary Roe, who stressed the importance of education. They urged him to obtain his master's degree in anthropology from Yale and a divinity degree from the Auburn Theological Seminary. He used their last name.

He named the institute in honor of his foster father, who died in 1911. School records indicate Cloud chose Wichita because of its central location.

Henry Roe Cloud was a graduate of Yale and listed in Who's Who in America.

The Roe Institute was north of what is now Wichita State University, at 3500 E. 21st. It included 100 acres of farmland, a lake, dairy barn, cottage, two halls and a bungalow. Tuition was $200 a year. Cloud hoped to attract more than 250 students, but no more than 40 a year attended.

The all-male school was one of the first American Indian high schools in the nation, with the majority of students coming from Oklahoma. It encouraged American Indians to assimilate into mainstream society.

"The aim of the school . . . is to train Indian boys for leadership of their own people," Cloud wrote in a pamphlet about the school. "This comes from the realization that the Indian must make his own way in a short time. If he is not trained for that time, he may suffer extermination. . . . The Indian must work himself into American civilization beside the white man and compete with him in intellect, manual ability and religious development."

Cloud's contribution was not without conflict, Washee said.

"One time, Mr. Cloud told us to forget that you are Indian. He said to make up your mind and try to be educated, be self-reliant. That created conflict. There were some boys who did not want to forget the Indian culture."

In 1931, the Bureau of Indian Affairs hired Cloud as a field representative. He was asked to strengthen ties between the BIA and the reservation-based American Indian communities. Although his school continued, he stepped down as director and turned the leadership over to the Presbyterian Board of Home Missions.

He was chosen in 1933 to be superintendent of Haskell Institute in Lawrence, the largest off-

The Roe Institute, north of Wichita State University, included 100 acres of land, a lake, a swimming pool, two halls and a bungalow. It closed in 1939.

lems. Its doors were closed in 1939, and the land was sold to Arthur and Marie Graber a year later. The land has since been parceled off and is developed with residential houses. The buildings were eventually razed, with the last—what was considered the administration building—torn down in 1990.

Cloud died in 1950 in Siletz, Ore. He had served as superintendent of the Umatilla Reservation at Pendleton, Ore. At the time of his death, he was tracing family histories to determine eligibility of Oregon coastal Indians for a $16 million lawsuit in payment of an early-day land seizure by the government.

In recognition of Cloud's achievements, Cloud Elementary School was named after him.

reservation high school run by the BIA. At Haskell, he introduced Indian-oriented courses into the curriculum.

During the 1930s, the American Indian Institute had financial prob-

Thurlow Lieurance

He turned Indian melodies into symphonies

When Thurlow Lieurance traveled to American Indian reservations shortly after the turn of the century, he liked what he heard.

So much, in fact, that he decided to preserve the Indians' music by putting it down on paper, recording it on early-day phonographs, and transforming portions of the traditional songs into symphony and orchestral music.

Lieurance brought the romance of the American Indian legend into his music, which was nationally known.

Lieurance, who was the dean of music at Wichita University, was an accomplished musician and composer. He became acquainted with American Indian music during periodic visits to his brother, Edward, a physician for the Crow reservation in Montana. The government then hired Lieurance to make Indian records, some of which are still in museums in Washington, D.C.

On one of the trips to visit his brother, Lieurance was badly injured.

He was on his way to the Little Big Horn when a team of horses he was driving ran away and overturned his wagon. Lieurance was trapped overnight under a dead horse, and his legs were exposed to freezing temperatures. He was permanently disabled by the accident, and he walked for the rest of his life with a crutch and a cane.

One of the songs he composed from his Montana trips, "By the Waters of the Minnetonka," brought him international fame.

On May 28, 1932, The Wichita Eagle reported:

"He heard the theme for the first time on an October evening in 1911 on the Little Big Horn across from the Custer battlefield. It was being played on a cedar flute by a young Sioux, Sitting Eagle."

The Eagle reported on Feb. 27, 1930, that the Damrosch Symphony Orchestra in New York was scheduled to play four songs Lieurance wrote in a suite called "Campfires."

"This is recognition of American music by an American composer," the article said. "It is fitting that he should be the one to bring forth American folk music. For years he has lived among the Indians at stated intervals, talked and sung

Thurlow Lieurance became acquainted with Indian music while visiting his brother, a physician for the Crow reservation in Montana.

with them through their ceremonials.

"He has taken into his heart their deep, reverent natures, nurtured by years and decades of a life close to the limitless stretches of land, the vastness of silent forests and the sounds of many waters."

Lieurance was born in Iowa on Sept. 7, 1878. His family soon moved to Neosho Falls, where he was reared. He was a bandmaster for the 22nd Kansas Volunteer Infantry in the Spanish-American War, becoming the youngest bandmaster in the war. He became head of the music department at Wichita University in 1927 and was granted a leave of absence in 1928 to study Indian music.

Lieurance was dean of music from 1926 to 1945, and he created more than 50 published works. In 1930, he composed "Minisa (Red Water at Sunset)," which won him the Presser Award at the Fountainbleu School of Music in France.

He died in September 1961 in Boulder, Colo.

William Dye

Grocer became the Chili King of the West

For almost seven decades, William Dye was known as the Chili King of the West.

He built an international businesses in Wichita on imported spices and peppers.

Dye began his career as a grocer at the turn of the century. By 1907, he had hit upon his specialty: supplying peppers, spices and seasonings to vendors who sold Mexican food to railroad workers.

Chili was a popular dish among the workers. Dye had been stocking chili-making supplies in his store since 1898. Among his imported spices were cumin, petine—a tiny, round, red, hot pepper—and oregano.

Local historians say that by 1908, Dye concentrated solely on the chili business. He built his first Mexican-food wholesale supply house, advertised nationally and distributed free samples to World War I American soldiers. At that time, Dye's chili factory was on the southwest corner of Washington and Douglas.

In 1923, he moved his factory to 120 N. Mosley.

Dye's son, Hubert, who joined the family-operated business in 1929, said the factory was the forerunner of fast-food businesses.

"My father was influenced by the large influx of Mexican people who came here because of the work on railroads," Hubert Dye said. "We sold a product that was readily available to the housewife.

"It was brick chili, which was 5 pounds of chili frozen into a brick form."

Dye, who lives in College Hill, said brick chili also was sold to small restaurants and hamburger stands.

"We had some customers buy hundreds of pounds of chili," he said. "The idea of selling chili and

William Dye was a Wichita grocer who became a fast-food entrepreneur with his chili.

"Juan, the Chili Kid" was Dye's company trademark. Dye created many of his company's sales slogans.

hamburgers went together."

The chili factory also produced a dry chili powder, which it shipped throughout the United States and exported to Canada, Mexico, Brazil, Peru, Argentine, the Philippines and other countries.

"Juan, the Chile Kid," was the Dye chili factory trademark. The design showed a small boy dressed in costume and leading a burro. Another version had him eating chili from a bowl. A 1962 Wichita Eagle article, which featured the chili factory, said Dye wrote many of the sales jingles used in his advertising.

The North Mosley building was the home of the Dye Chili factory until 1972, when William Dye died and the business was closed. Today, the building is used as a warehouse for computer supplies.

Wichita's Black Business District

For decades, minority businesses thrived

More than a decade after the Civil War, Southern blacks were drawn to Kansas, not only for its political climate as a free state but also for its promise of economic prosperity.

By the late 1870s, many of them had settled in Wichita, and between the 1880s and 1950s, a black business district thrived in an area roughly bounded by Central, Murdock, Main and Wichita.

Black business leaders say the district started to decline in the

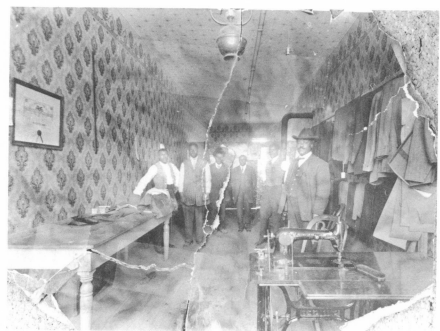

Charlie Patton's Tailor Shop at 633½ N. Main was part of the black business district around 1918. The district began to decline in the 1950s as businesses were forced to relocate.

Benjamin "Pap" Singleton became known as the father of Kansas black immigration.

1950s, when the city Urban Renewal Agency forced businesses to relocate so the Sedgwick County Courthouse could be built.

"Some of those businesses never fully recovered after that," said George T. Johnson, a former board member of the First National Black Historical Society of Kansas.

But in the 1880s, the businesses were growing, thanks to the immigration of thousands of southern blacks.

Many encouraged migration to Kansas, but a former Tennessee slave, Benjamin "Pap" Singleton, became famous for his efforts. He was convinced that blacks could not prosper in their old slave states and began recruiting them to Kansas during the 1870s, said John Gaston, associate professor of minority studies at Wichita State University.

Singleton became known as the "father of Kansas black immigration."

"Many came with the intent of establishing all-black towns; others were drawn to existing cities such as Kansas City, Lawrence, Leavenworth, Topeka and Wichita," Gaston said.

For blacks with little money, the cities often were their first stop.

"Many of these would-be farmers would obtain jobs in the cities and abandon their dreams of farming," Gaston said. "Others would move to the black towns or become farmers only to become victims of crop failures and harsh economic times and be forced to migrate back to the larger cities to find employment."

By the late 1880s, Wichita's black business district was beginning to take shape, Gaston said. From the late 1920s to the 1940s, businesses included Jackson Mortuary, Thompson Drug Store, Henry Carter's Dry Cleaners, Reed's Pool Hall, Oklahoma Cafe and Hotel, Link Henry's Barber Shop and Boxing Gym, and the Van Leu building, which had offices for doctors, attorneys and real estate agents.

Johnson recalls the district during its heyday.

"If you were driving down the street, you would see a lot of activity," he said. "And businesses were bustling. It was like a meeting area for the blacks."

Today, only two buildings remain from the business district: Calvary Baptist Church, 601 N. Water, and the Arkansas Valley Lodge, 615 N. Main. Both are local, state and national landmarks.

When the black businesses were moved from downtown, Johnson said, it dealt a heavy blow to the community.

"We really don't have an area where there is a large concentration of diversified black businesses," he said. "With integration and competition, it makes it hard for the black businessman to succeed."

Hotels,
Cathedrals
and Skyscrapers

*"It is my unprejudiced opinion that
there is no other hotel in the country
which can offer furnishings to compare
with those found in the Allis."*
—Barney Allis,
originator of the Allis Hotel

The Occidental Hotel

Stylish building has been turning heads for decades

Wichita turned out on the night the Occidental Hotel opened.

"There has not been since the laying of the foundations of our city, an occurrence that attracted more attention, created more good feeling, a subject of so much talk, and finally transpiring with so much real enjoyment as the grand opening of the Occidental," The Wichita Beacon reported.

That was 116 years ago. To some extent, the Occidental is still turning heads.

"It's a beautiful building with a unique style," said Linda Ayala, president of Realty Title Co., one of the businesses in the Occidental at 300 N. Main.

It's the oldest brick building in Wichita.

The hotel was built in 1874. The idea for it was planted in January 1873. A group of local investors and developers contributed to its construction.

It played a vital role in the development of the Southwest. Cattle barons, statesmen, politicians and celebrities signed its register for lodging.

Some of the more noted lodgers included Army Maj. Gen. Phil Sheridan, Chisholm Train supporter Joseph McCoy and outlaw Frank James.

The Wichita Beacon reported in its Jan. 21, 1874, story that the Occidental was furnished in style.

"Every room is fitted with fine ingrain carpet, spring beds, bedsteads of the newest design, elegant washstands, mirror, lounge and full

Outlaw Frank James was among the guests at the Occidental Hotel.

chamber sets."

But one of the most outstanding features of the hotel was the bridal chamber. It "is as elegant and tasteful as a Turkish Harem, to gaze upon it leaves a nameless longing in every married breast to be married over again, if for no other reason than the privilege of occupying this handsome little boudoir on the occasion."

In 1880, Emma Houston of Winfield purchased the hotel, hoping to convert it into a seminary or a private boarding school. But the plan was abandoned due to a lack of local enthusiasm.

Nevertheless, the building was overhauled. A new roof was constructed, shutters were put up, and new furnishings installed. In the middle 1880s, a veranda was

added.

By the turn of the century, the Occidental had been renamed the Baltimore and an east wing added. The hotel's front was "modernized" and its shutters and veranda removed. Dockum Drug leased the corner store of the hotel in 1930 and operated there for nearly three decades. In 1945, Luis Casado, a Wichita real estate agent, purchased the Baltimore for his firm.

Ken Wagnon, owner of Capital Enterprises Inc., and Bob Geist bought and restored the building in 1979, giving it back its original name.

"I was just fascinated with old buildings, and the Occidental was the first beautiful building in Wichita," Wagnon said.

The Carey-Eaton Hotel

Elegant and flashy, it was the pride of Wichita

John Carey was already known as a staunch Irishman who believed in Wichita and supported most of the town's early development. So in January 1886, when he announced plans to build a fine hotel, residents knew it would be flashy and elegant.

They were not disappointed.

Included in the design for the hotel to be situated on the southwest corner of St. Francis and Douglas were a steam-powered elevator, steam heat, hot and cold water for rooms, electric bells for guests and a huge dining room.

Carey came to Wichita in 1874 and became prominent through his lumber company and his land and livestock investments. The Wichita Eagle reported on Feb. 17, 1876:

"Mr. J.B. Carey shipped last Friday 43 fat hogs to Kansas City, which Barse & Snider sold in that market for $7.50 per hundred. The hogs averaged close upon 400 pounds per head, and the price realized was the highest of any lot of this season. Thirty dollars per head for hogs is at least a living price, besides the transaction leaves Sedgwick County ahead. Mr. Carey is an old and experienced dealer in hogs."

During the city's boom period of the 1880s, Carey's businesses and farms flourished, in part because he insisted on "honest dealings."

In his dealings, Carey was considered an honest person with a reputation of not cheating anyone, almost to the point of feeling religious about it. That may have been what advanced him later in politics.

It was during the boom period that Carey announced plans for the "finest hotel in the southwest." A Chinese laundry operator, Charlie Sing, was forced to relocate and several other buildings on the property were sold in 1886 and moved away to make room for the hotel.

On Oct. 18, 1887, The Wichita Daily Beacon reported that work on the Hotel Carey was progressing and that "all the furniture will be purchased in this city at a cost of $80,000. The house will be opened to the public about Dec. 1. It is already one of the best advertised houses in the west. The lessees are practical hotel men and will leave nothing undone to make the Carey the pride of the southwest."

It was billed as one of the finest, more exclusive hotels between St. Louis and Denver.

The hotel was a success, and three years later Carey became the city's ninth mayor. During his term, a new City Hall was completed and the features of Carey's face were chiseled in stone and placed to the right of the north entrance. The City Hall is now the Wichita-Sedgwick County Historical Museum, 204 S. Main.

Carey died on Nov. 19, 1899, in San Jose, Calif.

Thirteen months after his death, Carry A. Nation walked down the hotel's basement stairs and attacked the saloon.

The building was later renamed the Eaton Hotel.

John Carey built what is now known as the Eaton Hotel.

Hotel Carey, at the southwest corner of Douglas and St. Francis, was considered one of the finest hotels between St. Louis and Denver.

Wichita Children's Home

Family crisis was the source of the shelter

My dear mother,

This is a sad time for me. Sunday papa came up here to the home and said that you had one more week in whether you were going to marry Dave or not. And mamma for our sake don't because if you do we children will have to part and maybe not see each other again nor you neither if you can't come down before Sunday. And if you will not marry we will get a little start of money and rent a little house and see if we can't get along all right and if necessary I will work myself to keep you and us. Mamma we could get along fine and have the nicest and happiest home we ever had if you will do as I say or we will have to go to a home to be adopted out by Sunday. If you don't do as I say, don't you think it would be best and we could be kept together and when I got a little bigger I could help and buy at a farm or lot and make us a home. I have told Mrs. Jackson some of my troubles and I expect she will help me out and will write too. Now think about this. Your heart couldn't ache like mine. I may never see you again or papa. I don't know. And remember I love

you better than I love my own life and will make your living if I can.

From your loving son,
Gerald Long.

That letter appeared in The Wichita Eagle on March 14, 1909. The only explanation offered was that the missive had been misdirected by a boy at the Wichita Children's Home and was reproduced as an example of circumstances the staff occasionally met. It also was printed to help raise money for a new home.

"Nothing is sadder than the breaking up of a little home through death or estrangement," The Eagle said in a comment with the letter. "It is the duty of every community to support homes for the . . . proper care of these little ones."

The idea for the Wichita Children's Home began on May 14, 1888, when a Wichita farmer, Oliver Heady, needed someone to care for his seven children.

His wife had just died and he was looking for someone to give 24-hour-a-day attention to his children.

His neighbor, Catherine B. Gar-

Catherine B. Garver came to the rescue of a widowed farmer.

ver, the mother of four children, came to his rescue. Heady told Garver that if she would help him through his crisis by caring for his children, he would be willing to donate a cow.

She did and asked other Wichita women to join her, and on Aug. 2, 1888, the Wichita Children's Home was founded.

The home, now an emergency shelter for children age 3 to 17, for many years functioned as an orphanage. It had several addresses before settling in at 3800 E. First in 1891. The home was a two-story clapboard house with a huge basement.

In 1906, The Eagle reported: "The Wichita Children's Home now shelters 38 children. They are housed in a large frame structure of 14 rooms and a basement, and the association is out of debt; but it takes a large sum of money to support the home as nearly all of the children now in the home are cared for at the expense of the association."

By then, the home's staff already was considering larger and newer

The Wichita Children's Home for a while was a two-story clapboard house with a huge basement at 3800 E. First. It moved to 810 N. Holyoke, where it still is.

accommodations. It wasn't until 1913, however, that a new structure was built.

It's still at 810 N. Holyoke. A brick building was replaced in 1964 by the present brick home.

A.A. Hyde, the inventor of Mentholatum, gave liberally toward the construction of the 1913 brick building. He also furnished two Bibles to each of the 118 children living in the new home. The home

had a separate hospital for children who had contagious diseases.

The Wichita Children's Home is the oldest charitable institution in Wichita.

The Central Building

10-story structure housed downtown's economic hopes

Times were bleak in 1929, when the Central Building was constructed. But city officials hoped the new 10-story structure would save downtown Wichita from the nation's economic bust.

Promoted as Kansas' largest office building and touted as a major drawing card for downtown business, the building was supposed to symbolize prosperity. It housed 28 office suites on each floor, and in early years included the Lukins Cafe, S.H. Archer Prescription Drugstore, Central States Building and Loan Co., the Billie Cain Barbershop, the Mouos Candy Shop, Spines Clothing Store and The Cigar.

Today, as the Century Plaza Building on the southwest corner of Douglas and Main, it faces demolition because it is empty.

After 62 years as a downtown structure, the building was closed in the summer of 1991. Downtown development plans propose razing the building and turning the property into a park.

That's a far cry from the hopes the building carried when it first opened. The building was promoted as one of the prime areas for business. It was surrounded by other office buildings that were quickly being filled. The Wichita Eagle quoted the city's building superintendent on April 9, 1929:

"Ninety-five percent of space in Wichita's modern fireproof buildings is occupied and at least two-thirds of the vacant space that existed the first of the year has been filled by tenants."

The building was designed and promoted by George Herman Siedhoff, a local contractor and real estate developer who also built what then were known as Wesley Hospital and the Hotel Broadview.

Siedhoff was born March 7, 1878, in St. Louis. He came to Wichita in 1917 and was president of the George H. Siedhoff Con-

The Central Building was opened in 1929. In the 1960s, its name was changed to Century Plaza. Downtown development plans call for it to be razed.

George Herman Siedhoff also built Wesley Hospital and the Hotel Broadview.

struction Co.; president of Broadview Hotel Co.; director of Braley Aircraft Co.; president of Supreme Propeller Co.; and vice president of the Braley School of Flying.

His home was in the Hotel Broadview at Douglas and Waco.

In 1927, Siedhoff proposed an office building. Several months later, an investment group of 31 of the city's top business leaders was formed to promote the building. The group included C.Q. Chandler, president of First National Bank, and Henry J. Allen, former Kansas governor and owner of The Wichita Beacon.

The original plans called for a 15-story skyscraper costing $1 million. The plans were modified later to 10 stories, costing $800,000.

Stores, shops and businesses at one time in the building included Crown Jewelry, Prestinger Typewriter Co., the Sibyl Hat Shop, the Arkla Gas Co. and Farm Credit Banks.

During the 1960s, land was cleared to the south and west of the building to make room for Century II and a new library. The Central Building changed its name to Century Plaza, and a modern facade was placed over the structure, covering the terra-cotta and grand entrances. A plaza and small park were built on the west side of the building.

But the interior of the building looks much the same as it did when the building opened. The walls and floors are polished marble, and the ceiling features elaborate plaster moldings. It boasts four brass-fronted elevators.

"The closing shuts down a very active building that sits as an anchor for downtown Wichita," Ellington said. "Historically, it was very vital to downtown itself and to the skyline. It is sad to know that there are rumors that this building may be razed. It was a well-built structure, both on the exterior and interior."

The Allis Hotel

With 350 rooms, it was the city's showplace

When Barney Allis was a child peddling newspapers on the streets of Kansas City, Mo., he came across a poem that spurred him to become a wealthy hotel magnate.

It was written by one of Kansas' leading statesmen, John J. Ingalls, who not only was a senator but also taught school, practiced law and edited newspapers in Fredonia, Coffeyville and Topeka.

Allis was so moved by the poem that in 1930—when he built a 17-story, 350-room-hotel in Wichita—he wanted to name the new hotel after Ingalls. But friends persuaded him to name the building after himself.

He did, but still insisted on naming a meeting room after Ingalls and filling it with the senator's portraits. Allis had the "Opportunity" poem printed on a parchment panel and

Barney Allis said that his hotel company would be "an active booster for the welfare of the entire city."

placed on the door leading into the room.

The Allis was a state-of-the-art hotel for that time. It was built with the influence of art deco and a tinge of streamlining.

Allis promised Wichitans that his hotel would be not only the city's

In its heyday, the Allis Hotel boasted three restaurants, a barbershop, beauty parlor and florist. Each room had a fan and a radio. The building has been closed since 1970.

Wichita Beacon on Aug. 25, 1929. "Wichita is now more than a casual stopping place. It is unlike the city which has only one or two railroads. Wichita is also the crossroads of the airlines. It occupies a foremost place in air travel."

Because of that, he said, his hotel would offer three restaurants, a barbershop, beauty parlor, laundry, florist shop and drugstore. In addition, each guest room had circulating ice-water fans and radios.

"It is my unprejudiced opinion," Allis told reporters in November 1930, "that there is no other hotel in the country which can offer furnishings to compare with those found in the Allis."

And for a time that was true; the Allis was the gathering place for politicians and entertainers. From 1930 until 1962, the Allis was the tallest building in Wichita. After that, the Wichita Plaza-Vickers Tower, now known as the Kansas State Bank building, claimed that title.

Allis and his parents moved to Kansas City from Poland when he was 2 years old. Poor as a child, he worked his way up from selling newspapers on street corners, to printer, to hotel owner.

In Allis' heyday, the Allis Hotel Co. operated the Connor Hotel in Joplin, Mo., and the Baltimore and Hotel Muehlebach in Kansas City, Mo.

Allis sold his Wichita hotel in 1955. It was owned by several hotel chains, including the Sheraton, before it was closed in 1970. It has not reopened and is one of several downtown buildings that in recent years have been left vacant as businesses leave.

When Allis died on April 17, 1962, local newspapers reported that he was considered a friend to presidents Truman and Eisenhower.

tallest building but a showplace as well. The building still stands in downtown Wichita, on the southeast corner of Broadway and William.

"The Allis Hotel Company is coming to Wichita to be a part of the city. It will be an active booster for the welfare of the entire city," Allis said in an interview with The

St. Mary's Cathedral

Church's opening drew people of all faiths

hen St. Mary's Cathedral opened its doors for its dedication in September 1912, the townspeople of Wichita poured in.

So did a cardinal, five archbish-ops and scores of bishops.

On that day, the entire town celebrated—Catholics and non-

A photograph from the 1950s shows the exterior of the cathedral.

The exterior columns of the north portico of St. Mary's Cathedral were originally part of the federal building in Chicago.

Catholics alike. There was a parade, Mass, reception and speeches at the Forum, Wichita forerunner of today's Century II.

"James Cardinal Gibbons, America's most distinguished Catholic, accompanied by many of the most learned and distinguished members of the hierarchy, arrived in Wichita," The Wichita Eagle reported on Sept. 19, 1912. "Wichita's reception of her distinguished guests was cordial and Wichita-like, and today the city is celebrating with pomp and splendor the dedication of Wichita's magnificent cathedral."

The cathedral still stands, drawing the faithful to services each week. For 78 years, it has been a mainstay on the Wichita skyline.

The idea for Wichita's cathedral began in 1887 when a bishop was appointed for Wichita. He was the Rev. James O'Reilly. But he died before he could be consecrated.

The new diocese, established in 1887, went a year without a bishop. In 1888, the Rev. John Hennessy was appointed. He served until 1920.

It was during his term, in 1890, that the land at Central and Broadway was purchased. But construction didn't begin until 1906.

Materials used included red granite from Oklahoma, limestone from Bedford, Ind., and polished green Minnesota marble for the interior columns supporting the roof. The exterior columns of the north portico were originally part of the federal building in Chicago. When that building was razed in 1893, Hennessy bought the pillars and had them transported to Wichita.

The columns lay out on the property for some time before the construction of the cathedral.

In 1912, when the church was finally dedicated, Wichita's enthusiasm remained high.

In an interview with an Eagle reporter, published on Sept. 19, 1912, Gibbons said he was pleased

Polished green Minnesota marble was used for the interior columns.

that the celebration of the cathedral was a civic event. Festivities included politicians, local business leaders and residents all taking part, even though Catholics at that time were a minority.

"It shows to me that you are not living in a narrow-minded or bigoted community," the cardinal said. "Your people have a broad outlook inspired by these great prairies and the great sky. I am happy to find so well developed in Kansas that spirit of fairness and toleration, which is a mark of true Americanism."

The Keen Kutter Building

Warehouse's massive clock tower is a landmark

One of the showiest buildings in Wichita's warehouse district is the Keen Kutter building.

Built in 1906, the four-story brick building with its massive clock tower now stands as a landmark in the city's skyline. It is on the north side of First Street between Rock Island and Mosley.

What makes it unique is its architectural styling and its massiveness. It is a wholesale house that's more ornate than the average.

The building lies within Wichita's old wholesale district, bordered by Douglas, Second, Mead and Mosley. The heyday of the district was from the 1880s to the 1930s, with 1910 the peak of activity.

While the warehouse was being constructed, town leaders were enthusiastic, and on Dec. 3, 1905, The Wichita Eagle reported:

"The building is not only a credit to Wichita but is an indication of the growth of this city as a commercial center. The fact that the largest hardware house in the world . . . has decided on this city in which to establish their branch house proves beyond a doubt that the facilities as a distributing point . . . have given Wichita its present place in the commercial world and cannot be equaled in this section of the country."

In 1906, the Morton-Simmons Hardware Co. opened in the building. It was a wholesale hardware business controlled by the Sim-

This photo of the Keen Kutter warehouse is from 1931 when the building was owned by the A.J. Harwi Hardware Co., which bought it from the Morton-Simmons Hardware Co.

mons Hardware Co. of St. Louis. The company's Keen Kutter brand name was painted prominently on the tower.

Morton-Simmons remained active in the hardware business until Oct. 1, 1929, when it was sold to the A.J. Harwi Hardware Co. In 1932, the Harwi head office was moved to Wichita, but by 1937, the company had closed operations in the city.

"The wholesale district is not the magnitude that it once was because we don't have rail traffic like we used to," Ellington said. "We shipped a lot of things in and out from that area."

The Keen Kutter building, now

vacant, is owned by The Coleman Co.

David Burk, a partner in Market Place Properties, the firm that is developing the Old Town Plaza farmers market, says the building is architecturally significant because of its Romanesque, classic and Gothic designs.

"It's unusual in that most warehouse buildings were built next to one another," Burk said. "This building did not abut another. It has windows all around."

Burk said Market Place Properties plans to refurbish the building to house condominiums and a Design Mart.

The Live Stock Exchange Building

Once-thriving stockyards now silent

For many years, a sometimes strong stench in northeast Wichita symbolized the smell of money.

That was when Wichita and the cattle market depended on one another, and the stockyards still thrived.

The old Live Stock Exchange Building, 701 E. 21st, was a lively center of business. A special streetcar line ferried people to the area because so much was going on there.

It was especially active from 1910 until about 1940, so residents in Wichita always got an aroma of the product. Many times when the north wind blew, the smell would spread all over town.

Wichita's long relationship with the cattle business began in 1868 when Texas cattlemen drove herds on the Chisholm Trail through Wichita to Abilene.

When the railroad came to town in 1872, cattle pens were constructed one block south of the Waterman and Santa Fe intersection.

Fifteen years later, the Wichita stockyards were built on 28 acres north of 18th and on both sides of Emporia.

Hog pens, cattle sheds and a

A disastrous fire destroyed the Dold Packing plant in 1901.

three-story brick exchange building were erected.

Jacob Dold & Sons opened a packing plant at 21st and Emporia. The day before the plant opened, the stockyards burned. They were rebuilt almost immediately.

Dold & Sons had competition when Francis Whittaker & Sons Packing Co. opened in 1890 at 21st and Topeka. Cudahy Packing Co. bought Whittaker in the mid-1890s.

The stockyards continued to operate north of 18th until the turn of the century, when the Wichita Union Stockyards were constructed on 10 acres east of Emporia on 21st Street. Then the old yards were closed.

One of Wichita's most disastrous fires occurred on July 16, 1901, when the Dold Packing plant was destroyed.

In 1909 the Live Stock Exchange Building at 701 E. 21st was constructed.

The exchange housed 15 livestock commission firms, a national bank, stockyard company offices, the Wichita Terminal Railway Co. and branch offices of the packing houses.

It was where people went to do business. There were barbershops, restaurants and stores. The commissioners came in and handled the transactions. It was a place where the farmers could shop when they came to town.

So active was northeast Wichita with the cattle market that a special streetcar line was built, The Stockyard Line.

And, in later years, Wichita residents became familiar with Bruce Behemyer, who gave daily market reports on KFH radio and ended his commentary with the sound of a

The Live Stock Exchange Building in more current times.

cowbell.

But more cattle yards and packing plants sprung up in western Kansas, and the demand for the facilities lessened in Wichita.

The Live Stock Exchange Building closed its cattle auction business in 1979.

The building was later reopened as a work-release center for Kansas prison inmates, but closed when the Oklahoma-based company that ran the center went bankrupt.

The building is now vacant.

The Caldwell-Murdock Building

Wife left lasting legacy to keep her husband's name alive

Louise Caldwell Murdock loved her husband.

So much so, she did all she could to ensure that the name Roland P. Murdock would be remembered.

In 1907, one year after his death, she had the first skyscraper in Wichita built and named it the Caldwell-Murdock Building, after her husband and her father, Jonathan Caldwell.

When she died eight years later, she left a trust fund for buying a city-owned art collection. The Roland P. Murdock collection later became the foundation of the Wichita Art Museum.

Shortly after her death, The Wichita Beacon on April 23, 1915, reported:

"Mrs. Murdock was, perhaps, one of the best businesswomen in Wichita. Soon after the death of her husband, she planned the seven-story Caldwell-Murdock Building as a memorial to his life and work. The building is one of the best office buildings in Wichita and is now a monument to herself and her devotion to her husband and the people of Wichita."

Originally from New York state, Louise Caldwell came to Wichita in 1871 with her parents. She was 14. Her father was a local grocer and located his business in the old Eagle Block, near the corner of Main and Douglas.

After attending public school in Wichita, she married Roland Murdock in 1877. Both were choir members at First Methodist Church.

Roland Murdock, brother of the founding editor of The Wichita Eagle, Marshall Murdock, was the paper's business manager.

Through the years, Louise Murdock was known for her cultural and intellectual interests. She was an enthusiastic supporter of the Chautauqua movement, which helped bring many nationally known speakers to Kansas.

In 1899, she helped begin the 20th Century Club and served as its first president. The club, which is still active, was designed to promote the arts, literature and other cultural interests.

After her husband's death in 1906, Louise Murdock went to New York and studied interior design.

The Caldwell-Murdock Building downtown, built in 1907, was Wichita's first skyscraper. It was a memorial to Roland P. Murdock and Jonathan Caldwell.

Charles Rollins/The Wichita Eagle

When she returned to Wichita, she became the state's first interior decorator and opened a studio in the Caldwell-Murdock Building.

She selected and designed the interiors for Wichita's Carnegie Library, now the Omnisphere & Science Center.

"It was pretty evident that she loved (her husband)," Ellington said. "That she went to those lengths, to name a building and art collection in memory of her husband, to me is the ultimate in terms

Louise Caldwell Murdock was called one of the city's best businesswomen.

of affection and respect."

Until recently, the Caldwell-Murdock Building at 111 and 113 E. Douglas housed offices and retail businesses. It is now one of several vacant buildings in downtown Wichita.

"It has ornate terra-cotta work running across the first and second levels of the building," said Dave Burk, past chairman of the Historic Preservation Board. "It's really spectacular. That feature alone is very unusual and would make it architecturally significant."

The Michigan Building

City's skinniest skyscraper soared to grandeur

It has been called Wichita's skinniest skyscraper.

Built in 1910, the Michigan building was the pride of Oscar Barnes, who erected the 25-foot-wide, six-story office building at 206 E. Douglas. At that time, it was touted as a skyscraper. Today, it houses Rector's Book Store.

Much of its grandeur has been lost because of the modern facade that's on the first two floors. But early on, it had a marquee above the entrance that gave it a lot of prestige.

Barnes was a pioneer druggist and music dealer who came to Wichita in 1879 from Kalamazoo, Mich. In addition to the Michigan, he built the Barnes Block building at the southeast corner of Broadway and Douglas.

Barnes was the uncle of Fred Ayers and the father of Maurice Barnes, proprietors of a men's clothing store that was the first business in the new Michigan building.

On April 1, 1910, The Wichita Eagle reported: "The fixtures are

The Michigan building, which now houses Rector's Book Store, was home to clothing and music stores in earlier days.

solid mahogany, inlaid with holly. Everything is either under glass or in drawers and cabinets. There are no hideous and unsightly cases and boxes. There are separate compartments for everything, the hosiery, shirts, neckwear, collars and general furnishings being in handsome mahogany cabinets or glass cases."

Eight years later, the building became the home of the Martin & Adams Music Co. In 1919, the name was changed to J.O. Adams Music Co., which operated there until 1930, when the name was again changed, this time to the Adams-Bennett Music Co. The music store closed in 1956, and the Michigan building housed the Holiday Shoe Store for the next decade. Several other businesses occupied the building before Rector's moved there in 1972.

The white-faced stone building has a classic style with a Greek influence. It was one of the first buildings in Wichita constructed of steel and one of the first to be fireproofed.

Barnes died in 1921.

All Hallows Academy

A prairie vision became a school

Little more than raw prairie stood on the spot where the Rev. M.J. Casey envisioned a Wichita school for girls.

He believed in his vision so much that in 1886, he traveled to Dubuque, Iowa, to talk with the Sisters of Charity of the Blessed Virgin Mary.

The sisters were known for their high quality of teaching, and he wanted teachers from the convent to staff the school.

Mother Superior Mary Frances Clarke refused, saying there were already too few teachers to meet the growing demand. But Casey

persisted in his wish for a school, and told the sisters he would remain in the convent parlor until they granted his wish.

Mother Clarke finally relented, and in 1887, sent four sisters to Wichita to start Casey's school. He named it All Hallows Academy after a school he had attended in Ireland. It was later renamed Mount Carmel.

"It gave Wichita the exclusive girls school that it probably needed," Ellington said. "There were several families that wanted finer education for their daughters. And All Hallows answered their concerns. Marshall Murdock used to send his daughter to the academy."

All Hallows Academy was at what is now 3100 W. Douglas. It contained a chapel, parlor, three classrooms, three music rooms, kitchen and laundry.

The sisters began planting rows of saplings on the grounds, and Casey expanded the campus to 68 acres, using donations and gifts from Wichita residents. In September 1887, the school opened with 21 students.

The only other educational institution in Wichita at the time was the Lewis Academy. Garfield University opened the same year as All Hallows. Of the three, only All Hallows continued until 1962 without a change in control.

The name All Hallows was changed to Mount Carmel at the turn of the century. In 1906, a chapel wing was added to provide study halls, a science laboratory, recreation parlors, a gymnasium, dormitories and a library.

In 1962, the academy was relocated to 8500 E. Central. From 1962 through 1964, the old building served as a boys high school and was known as Notre Dame. The boys left the building when Bishop Mark K. Carroll High School was built at 8101 W. Central.

The All Hallows/Mount Carmel Academy was noted for its 50-foot cedar trees and small lake spanned

All Hallows Academy was at what is now 3100 W. Douglas.

All Hallows Academy opened with 21 students in 1887. The school, named by the Rev. M.J. Casey, became Mount Carmel.

by an arched foot bridge. In 1965, the building was razed so that the property could be sold.

Today all that remains of the name All Hallows is a street in west Wichita.

Lewis Academy

Private school drew the city's elite

Ellen Snyder remembers all too well the days when she was a student at the Lewis Academy.

Snyder attended the private school in the late 1890s from age 7 through the eighth grade. It was one of Wichita's first private schools, competing with All Hallows Academy. The huge, three-story brick building stood near the southeast corner of Third and Mar-

Hiram Lewis came to Wichita in 1876 and established the Farmers and Merchants Bank, which now is First National Bank.

In 1908, the Lewis Academy was moved to Emporia and became the Lewis Hall of Science at the College of Emporia.

ket, where the YWCA parking lot is.

"It was not exactly exclusive," Snyder said. "But the elite of Wichita did go to school there. We had Bible study classes and gymnasium classes. We learned ethics and the spiritual side of life. We learned to care for our bodies there."

The academy was named for Hiram Lewis, an early Wichita banker. The building was known as the Wichita Academy when it was built in 1886. That year, though, Lewis endowed the school with $25,000, and almost immediately, the name was changed.

The academy was successful. It was known for its high ideals and competent teaching staff.

The Lewis Academy operated for almost 20 years. In 1908, the school was moved to Emporia and became the Lewis Hall of Science at the College of Emporia. The building later became Wichita's YWCA.

Throughout the school's existence, it placed strong emphasis on religion.

Old school records show that in 1887, "There were 273 graduates. Of these, the number of professing Christians at the time of graduation was 233."

Lewis, in fact, was well-known for his charitable contributions to local churches and religious associations, such as the YMCA.

Lewis was born March 11, 1843, near Warren, Ohio. He fought on the Union side in the Civil War, serving in the Ohio Volunteer Infantry. He was wounded in the wrist by buckshot during a battle at Chickamauga, Ga.

In 1869, he went to Mississippi to manage a plantation owned by his father. He became active in politics and was elected to the Mississippi Legislature in 1870. He edited the Columbus Press from 1871 to 1876 and was a county sheriff.

In 1876, Lewis came to Wichita, where he established the Farmers and Merchants Bank. Later the name of the bank was changed to Kansas National Bank, now the

First National Bank. He also was president of the National Loan Co., president of the First National Bank of Pratt, and vice president of the Kingman National Bank.

Lewis was known for his intellectualism. He wrote and was considered to be thought-provoking. He was a mentor for a lot of people. People sought him out for financial and spiritual guidance, Ellington said.

When Wichita went bust in 1889, Lewis was one of the surviving capitalists who continued to buy land, believing the town would someday rebound. He was quoted in The Wichita Eagle:

"Times do seem a little hard, but do you know that if you were to wipe out every vestige of this town, the pavement, the sidewalks and all the buildings, clean it all out and leave this people here with the bare ground but out of debt, soon they would build a great city."

Lewis died in 1912.

The Kansas Sanitarium

Place of mystery provided a "restful retreat"

The Kansas Sanitarium was a place of mystery for those who didn't go inside its doors.

Located away from city noises, it offered a quiet solitude for those needing rest or medical help.

Beginning in 1903, people flocked to its doors.

The idea for a sanitarium started in 1902, when the Nebraska Sanitarium in Lincoln sent two registered nurses to Wichita. Their treatments consisted of diet, exercise, massage, hot and cold sprays, and electrical therapy.

The treatments became so popular that a sanitarium was built to serve Wichita residents. A four-story brick building was constructed in 1903 at what is now the 3400 block of West Douglas.

The Kansas Sanitarium then billed itself as a "restful retreat for both medical and surgical patients."

Most of the people who went there were middle- and upper-class who considered it a luxury.

The sanitarium's 1909 annual report stated that the patronage was good; that the financial condition of the institution was in good order; and that 22 nurses were in training. In 1911, as many as 50 patients were crowded into the institution.

The sanitarium continued growing and at its peak, in 1917, more than 1,000 patients were treated.

But during the middle 1920s, the patronage began declining, parti-

In 1911, as many as 50 patients were crowded into the Kansas Sanitarium, which emphasized diet and rest.

ally because of management. There was a constant turnover of superintendents. And, on Oct. 16, 1928, the sanitarium was closed.

The building sat vacant for two years. One Sunday morning in February 1930, The Wichita Eagle reported that the sanitarium building had been sold to J.S. Porter and the Rajah Rabbitry.

"Thanks to J.S. Porter, Wichita seems to be well on its way to becoming the Rabbit Capital of the World," the paper said.

Six months later Porter packed his personal belongings and left mysteriously in the night, leaving

hundreds of starving rabbits in the old building.

Finally, on Oct. 30, 1930, the building was sold to Sedgwick County and became the county hospital. The nurses' home from the sanitarium days, which was also on the institution's ground, was used for the poor farm, where the needy were cared for at public expense.

The building was razed several decades ago. Today, the property is part of West Douglas Park.

The sanitarium served as a forerunner of Wichita's present hospital system.

Eccentrics,
Sea Captains
and Recluses

"I'm an old man; I can't move very well, judge. The reason is because my underwear is too tight."
—*"Durable" Del Crozier*

Cannonball Green

Speed and diamonds were his signature

Without a doubt, Cannonball Green had style.

Legend has it that the frontier stagecoach owner and driver could take his whip and flick a fly off his lead horse without startling the animal. A huge, burly man, he based his reputation on flashing diamonds, fast horses and ingenuity.

Even as he lived there was always a little bit of mystery about him. He was outgoing. He colored the lore of the West and at the same time provided meaningful transportation in the development of the West.

Donald Robertson Green was born in Clinton County, Ky., in 1839. Lured by opportunities in southwestern Kansas, Green brought a herd of thoroughbred horses and coaches to the Wichita area in 1882 and began the Cannonball Stage Co.

Green worked in and out of Wichita on the theory that settlers coming to the end of the city's railroad line would hire him to take them by stagecoach to their claims farther west.

He was right.

Within a few years, his popularity had spread and, according to the book "The War Chief" by John Frizzell, Green was soon wearing

Cannonball Green could use a whip to flick a fly from a horse without startling the animal.

diamonds and boasting "that he owned more diamonds than were owned altogether west of the Mississippi by all other would-be diamond owners."

Green was 44 when he came to Wichita. He purchased a small livery stable and office and started his empire. He advertised for business and began scheduled runs from Wichita to Kingman and Coldwater. His teams and coaches could make the run in about 10 hours, with re-

lay stops every 20 miles.

Marshall Murdock, a close friend and founding editor of The Wichita Eagle, gave him a contract to carry the newspaper to outlying towns. Green also carried the mail.

His stagecoach route was known as the Cannonball Highway. It started on what is now West Street and ran west along Maple for 11 miles, turned south for one mile, then hooked up with what is now U.S. 54 west to Kingman.

His stage line helped build towns such as Garden City, Leoti, Meade, Pratt and Greensburg. The latter was named after him.

Green left Wichita in 1893 and moved to Oklahoma, where he hoped to establish the same type of stagecoach line. But the nation's economic depression in the '90s left him in poverty.

"The fact that he initially started the transportation development in this part of the area west of Wichita is an inspiration," Ellington said. "Without him? I'm sure there might have been another carrier that would have come to the front who might have accomplished as much as he did, but not as colorful."

Cannonball Green died in 1922 in Long Beach, Calif. He is buried in Wichita's Maple Grove Cemetery.

Father Bliss

Illiterate dentist treasured others' castoffs

People about town called him Father Bliss.

An elderly, illiterate dentist, he had a reputation in Wichita as an eccentric character who liked to decorate his house with other people's castoffs.

His house was filled with oddities. "Dr. Bliss made his abode, soon filling it with buffalo horns, tinware, paper, rags, bones, bottles

and an assortment of terrestrial refuse, only equalled by the old curiosity shop described by Charles Dickens," The Wichita Eagle reported Feb. 17, 1889.

But Silas Bliss was more than a local curiosity. He is remembered for his ingenuity in turning trash into something of value.

A local deacon told The Wichita Beacon after Bliss died in 1889 that

a resident had once made fun of Bliss' collection, and it so upset Bliss that he challenged the visitor to find one worthless object. The man looked around and picked out a broken tumbler.

Bliss took the broken glass and said: "Ye see this thick round part at the bottom? Now I will break all the glass away from the top, leaving only the thick part. This will make

A conceptual drawing shows Silas Bliss as Bill Ellington envisions him. Bliss was one of the first dentists in the area.

an excellent magnifying glass, such as cannot be excelled in power at the cost of this."

The earliest record of Bliss' stay in Wichita was in 1870, when he was listed in the city directory as a 70-year-old white male. A dentist from New York, he could neither read nor write.

His illiteracy didn't seem to matter, though. Most of the other Wichita residents at that time couldn't read or write, either.

What did matter was that he was a well-respected professional. He was a well-known fixture in the community.

Bliss' dental office was at the corner of First and Main. He was one of the first dentists in the region.

The Eagle reported in 1889: "One bright spot in the doctor's life to which he referred with pride was his early connection with the American Dental Association, having been the first president of the society."

The newspaper may have been wrong, Ellington said; there is no proof that Bliss was ever president of the ADA.

But there was little doubt about his creativity. A.A. Hyde, the founder and inventor of Mentholatum, marveled at it in a Feb. 18, 1889, article in The Wichita Beacon:

"I went to his room, and among all the other piles of odds and ends that the old man had picked up was a pile of old circus posters. I asked him what on earth he was doing with all that trash in his room. The old man grew indignant at hearing me call that stuff trash and at once explained to me the use to which he could put those old circus posters.

" 'I can cut out these big letters. . . . They can be used in the schools to teach children the alphabet. There is no better way to teach them than by the use of those big letters. Don't call these things trash; there is nothing that exists that is

not good for something.' "

Records from the Maple Grove Cemetery show that Bliss died of old age in February 1889. He was 89 years old.

So moved were the local residents by his death, that they set about raising funds for a memorial urn. An article from The Eagle on Feb. 16, 1889, reported that "The Eagle will receive funds for the erection of a marble slab to be placed over Father Bliss' grave. We do not wish to limit the amount but would prefer that 25 cents be the limit. In this way all who desire can contribute any amount from 25 cents down. This will give the old settlers, the business man, the church members, the children an opportunity. It is in the reach of all."

Eric Cale, manager of the Maple Grove Cemetery where Bliss is buried, said an iron urn on a limestone base and platform was erected on Bliss' grave. The urn is missing, but cemetery officials are restoring another urn of the same era to be placed on the grave.

He may have been eccentric. He was certainly peculiar. But the townspeople loved him.

"He was called father because of his age," Ellington said. "He was a sage, a very interesting old sage. Everyone sort of looked up to him as an aged fixture of the community."

Edwin Rutherford Powell

Sea captain took over the helm of mule-drawn streetcars

When Edwin Rutherford Powell arrived in the Wichita area in the 1870s, townspeople were excited to have a sea captain among their ranks.

Powell, local papers reported, was the first American captain to sail around Cape Horn. They said he navigated the cape while sailing from Maine to California, after gold was discovered in California in 1849.

It wasn't until the early 1870s that Powell left the shipping business and arrived in Augusta to start a general merchandise store.

City leaders built tracks to sections of town they wanted to promote, so the mule-drawn cars fueled city growth.

Edwin Rutherford Powell also served as Fourth National Bank president.

A decade later, he moved to Wichita and bought the city's first street railway with mule-drawn cars.

"Besides being a thorough businessman, Capt. Powell is a very pleasant, genial gentleman, possessing in a large degree the warmhearted sociability of the sailor, he having been for years captain of a large ocean vessel," The Wichita Eagle reported on Aug. 29, 1884. "We take pleasure in welcoming the captain to the queen city of the valley, and wish him much prosperity in conducting the street railway."

Local historians say the mule-car railway started a local industrial revolution.

"It started the actual real estate growth in the city," Ellington said. "It was very common back then that when city leaders wanted to promote a section, they would lay out a new streetcar system to that area. The developers worked very closely with the street railway people. Almost all sections of the town were eventually serviced by the street railway system."

Powell also became president of Wichita's Fourth National Bank. The Eagle reported that in the summer of '90, with Wichita in an economic bust that had started the year before, residents made a run on the bank. There was $40,000 on deposit and only $3,000 cash on hand, and people were lined up at the window.

Ellington said the bank's customers weren't causing a riot, but they were demanding their money.

"Once they were reassured the bank was solvent, it squelched all their apprehension."

Powell was reported to have gathered the bank's securities, dashed to Kansas City and talked with several financiers. They guaranteed the depositors' accounts, and the bank was saved.

But Powell was best known for his work with the mule-car system, which grew significantly under his command. When he took it over, it had a two-mile radius through downtown Wichita, and under his leadership, 64 miles were added.

Ironically, it was that streetcar system that caused his death. At that time, Powell was owner of the Crystal Ice Co.

On May 9, 1902, Powell was delivering a block of ice at a home north of Topeka and Third. He had completed the delivery and was climbing back into his buggy when he dropped the reins, which frightened his horse. The horse bolted, and when Powell pulled on the second rein, the horse turned suddenly, throwing him from the buggy. He fell headfirst onto the streetcar track.

Dan Cupp

He left Wichita for Towanda and a sharp-tongued woman

Dan Cupp, an early-day trader and postmaster, could have owned the center of Wichita, but instead he chose to homestead near Towanda and marry the "meanest woman in Butler County."

In the spring of 1860, Cupp drove his wagon over what is now Douglas Avenue and decided that the land surrounding the junction of the two rivers was nothing but sandy swampland.

Cupp's family members still talk about his choice.

"I can't say that we were upset about his decision," said Catharine Walker, a granddaughter who lives in Haverhill. "Back then, there wasn't any settlement. But it would have been nice if he would have chosen it."

Cupp married Sarah Malan in September 1861 and homesteaded a claim 1½ miles north of where Towanda stands. He sold the property when the Civil War broke out and enlisted in the 17th Kansas regiment. He was honorably discharged at Fort Leavenworth in December 1864.

Cupp worked as a blacksmith near Junction City until 1866. He returned to Towanda and homesteaded a 130-acre claim one-half mile northwest of town. He also served as the town's postmaster.

Family members say Sarah Cupp was known for her colorful personality.

"She was quite temperamental and real sharp-tongued," Walker recalled.

Old newspaper accounts indicate that Sarah Cupp was a skilled hunter, capable of shooting wild game near the cabin.

"On one occasion she shot a wild turkey, which proved to be a 21-pound gobbler," an edition of The Wichita Eagle said. "She has also fought off wildcats that were carrying away her chickens."

Glenda Everett, a great-great-granddaughter of the Cupps who lives in south Wichita, said Sarah had the reputation of being the

Dan Cupp thought the area near the confluence was sandy swampland.

Sarah Cupp was a skilled hunter, according to newspaper accounts, and bagged a 21-pound turkey. She also fought off wildcats carrying away her chickens.

"meanest woman in Butler Country." Everett said one family story revolves around Sarah's tongue.

"She didn't like one of her sons' wife," Everett said. "She told him, 'There you flitted around all the butterflies and landed on a horse. . . .' "

Cupp traded with the Comanches, Cheyennes, Arapahos, Kiowas and Apaches and carried a bear claw on a watch fob. The claw came from a bear that he killed near Hutchinson.

"Mr. Cupp traveled all over the state bartering calico, tinware, copper wire and cheap trinkets for buf-falo robes," The Eagle reported in November 1925. "On one of these trips he killed a bear on the Salt Plains near Hutchinson and witnessed a scalp dance. . . . The veteran trader wears an inch-and-a-half claw as a souvenir of the kill."

Another Eagle article reported a meeting Cupp had with two strangers during the 1870s. They rode up one night as he was doing chores and asked if they could spend the night.

"Sure you can," responded Cupp, "if you don't growl at the grub!"

The men ate dinner, chatted until bedtime, slept and ate breakfast the next morning. As they were getting ready to ride away, one of the men offered Cupp $2 for his hospitality.

Cupp refused and was then asked by the strangers if he knew who they were. He said he didn't.

"Well, if anybody should happen to ask you, tell them that we are Jesse James and Bob Younger."

The Cupps had 10 children. Sarah died in the 1920s, Dan in 1930.

The Cupps' homestead is still farmland; the foundations of the house and the barn are all that remain.

George Litzenberg

The newspaper columns of "Farmer Doolittle" were a favorite

The top headlines of The Wichita Eagle's Feb. 20, 1913, edition boast "Farmer Doolittle Off for Washington."

"Wichita Eagle's Famous Pioneer Reporter Who Began With the Paper in 1872 Goes to Visit Scenes of Childhood and See Wilson Properly Inagurated."

In the winter of 1913, George Litzenberg was 75 years old. But not many people in the area knew him by that name. He was better known as Farmer Doolittle.

Farmer Doolittle's career as a Kansas journalist began in 1872 when Marshall Murdock, founding editor of The Wichita Eagle, was searching for a columnist and met Litzenberg, a pioneer settler from Mulvane.

Using the pen name Farmer Doolittle, Litzenberg began a series of quaint writings, telling of the neighborhood gossip around Dog Creek, which became famous in pioneer journalism as the "Dog Creek News." The column ran once a week from 1872 until the late 1880s.

"He was an inspiration for all because of the way he wrote about areas," Ellington said. "He had an

George Litzenberg wrote under the pen name Farmer Doolittle.

enthusiasm that was quite unique. He did more than say Farmer Jones put in a crop of corn. He would note the significance of why. Maybe he was our first in-depth reporter.''

When Litzenberg started writing for The Eagle, the newspaper was at Main and Douglas, where the Hardage Center is today. The Eagle Block Building housed the newspaper until 1884, when the business was moved next door to a new three-story building, now the site of the Caldwell-Murdock Building. In 1908, a new Eagle building was constructed at the southwest corner of Market and William.

In 1910, Litzenberg contributed an article for a book titled ''History of Sedgwick County.'' In it he

stated: ''Wichita people know that this city is growing and they are firm in the belief that the Peerless Princess is now and will continue to be the 'Gateway to the Great Southwest.'

''There is, however, one pleasing feature of the growth of Wichita that a great many people overlook, and that is the growth of surrounding towns. A great city is always surrounded by large towns.''

In 1921, Victor Murdock, Col. Murdock's son, was running the paper and described Litzenberg as a reporter who would often hold up political meetings by rearranging the items on his desk and disposing of his hat and overshoes.

Charles Payne

Animal collector crusaded for the rights of wildlife

Long before there was widespread public interest in cancer research or animal rights, Wichita's Charles Payne was crusading.

Born in Kentucky in 1852, Payne came to Wichita during the boom period of 1886 and became affluent by investing in real estate. When the city's bust came in 1889, he was left penniless. At that time, he began pursuing the study of nature.

He began collecting all types of animals. During the 1890s, Payne made a living and gained some no-

Naturalist Charles Payne had a menagerie called Payne's Paradise, where Lawrence-Dumont Stadium is now; the menagerie was the forerunner of the Sedgwick County Zoo.

Charles Payne made a living in the 1890s by catching jackrabbits.

toriety by catching jackrabbits and shipping them all over the world for coursing meets. His rabbit roundups involved stretching nets across two sides of a field and using volunteers to drive the rabbits into the nets.

Payne's business of shipping live animals to various parts of the world included everything from a kangaroo mouse to a buffalo. At one time, he was the largest collec-

tor of North American animals and birds in the country, according to the ''History of Wichita and Sedgwick County Kansas,'' published by O.H. Bentley in 1910.

But Payne kept some of the animals in Wichita and had a menagerie called Payne's Paradise in Payne's Pasture, located at what is now Lawrence-Dumont Stadium. That menagerie was the forerunner of the Sedgwick County Zoo.

Payne also established several animal farms for fur-bearing animals and applied for a patent on a humane animal and bird trap that did not maim the animal or bird caught in it.

Nationally, he was known as a contributor to scientific and sportsman's journals.

He copyrighted a set of rules for a successful life and formed a research association for discovering a cure for cancer. And when he believed he had found a remedy, he took out a charter in the state of Kansas and planned to give the treatment free to the public.

"He was a bit of a different drummer," Ellington said. "People looked at him with awe. He was a flamboyant-looking fellow who had a dramatic appearance about him."

In an interview with Payne published in 1928, The Wichita Eagle Sunday Magazine quoted him as saying:

"Every man carries within him the potentialities of perfection of his spiritual, mental and physical self. The creation of life is the most sacred and beautiful of all gifts bestowed upon man."

Payne died on July 24, 1944. He was 92.

J. Hudson and Eva McKnight

Rich cultural legacy emerged after wife's death

J. Hudson and Eva McKnight were one of the wealthiest couples in Wichita at the turn of the century.

During their early years in the city, they were active and well-liked. Then they went into self-imposed exile.

Local historians and records indicate that a combination of reasons—including politics, taxes and a mentally retarded son—prompted the McKnights' change.

"To me, it's a rather pathetic tale of a family who was always respected," Ellington said. "They were outgoing until the child was born, and then they became very protective of him. Mr. McKnight was set in his ways," and Eva McKnight followed his lead, although she eulogized him through community services after his death.

Her legacy includes the McKnight Art Center at Wichita State University.

In 1884, J. Hudson McKnight brought his bride to Wichita. He was 25 and she was 23.

They were well-liked in the community.

Eva McKnight was well-educated in art and music, and became involved in cultural activities in the city. J. Hudson McKnight was active in the civic affairs of the city and gave generously of his time. He was considered to be a self-made man.

J. Hudson McKnight established a wholesale hardware company, the

J. Hudson and Eva McKnight were wealthy recluses at the turn of the century.

McKnight Cutlery Co., at 352 N. Main. In 1896, McKnight bought the Robert Black farm at a public auction. The land—bounded by what are now Douglas, Hydraulic, Kellogg and Grove—cost McKnight only a few thousand dollars.

In 1897, the couple built a home at 200 S. Hydraulic and named it Willowdale Place.

As the town grew, J. Hudson McKnight was determined to keep his land, but he began to feel the city encroaching. The property around his holdings was subdivided and sold for homes. As the residential developments grew, McKnight was taxed for sewers, street paving, sidewalks and the dredging and straightening of

Chisholm Creek, which ran through his property.

He became bitter, convinced the city was trying to take his land.

"When his tax case came before the court, he presented an impressive appeal to the opposition," Ellington said. "McKnight represented himself, for he trusted no one to take his case."

His distrust of fellow Wichitans was strengthened when, in 1909, he established The State Mutual Savings Bank. It ended in failure the same year, Ellington said.

"The closing wasn't due to Mr. McKnight's inexperience in financial matters, but his established image to the townspeople," Ellington said.

Mike Hutmacher/The Wichita Eagle

A trust fund set up by Eva McKnight led to the construction of McKnight Art Center at Wichita State University.

In the early 1920s, Wichita needed land for a new high school, and the eastern portion of McKnight's property—the area extending east of the canal to Grove—was considered an ideal location. The City Commission condemned the land for this purpose.

"He felt he had been robbed by the city," Ellington said.

The family continued to live in silence, apart from the community. When J. Hudson McKnight died on Aug. 19, 1925, Eva McKnight resumed her active life, rejoining civic organizations.

Before she died in 1927, she instructed her attorneys to draw up an estate that would provide the city with various educational and cultural gifts, Ellington said. One of the first gifts was to establish the McKnight Memorial Fountain, which features a statue of a trailblazer and an Indian, at East High School. She also set up a trust fund that eventually was used to build McKnight Art Center.

Her gesture surprised the community.

"The community respected her immensely. But almost everyone who knew the family knew that she respected her husband enough to endure the oddities that he instilled," he said. "She chose to live his lifestyle."

Their son, George, died in 1969, the same year the huge limestone house with ornate fretwork, turrets, colored glass and porch swing was razed.

Bliss Isely

Author, historian was plagued by poor health

People used to talk about Bliss Isely.

A writer of Kansas history and government, a former newspaperman and publicist, Isely was well-known in Wichita's social circles. So well-known that area residents were often concerned about his health. He battled for years against tuberculosis, a hemorrhage in his lungs and Parkinson's disease.

"He looked like he was going to die the next minute," said Jerry Clark, photographer at The Wichita Eagle, of the days when Isely would come to The Wichita Beacon's office to deliver stories from the Wichita Chamber of Commerce.

Nevertheless, Isely "lived another 20 years," Clark recalled.

Isely's passion was history. His first book was written in 1927: "Early Days in Kansas."

During his career he wrote other books, which included "Blazing the Way West," "Four Centuries in Kansas," "The Story of Kansas," "Kansas Civil Government," "Our Careers as Citizens," "Sunbonnet Days" and "Our Presidents, Men of Faith."

His last book, "The Horsemen of Shenandoah," was published in November 1963.

"As a historian, he left his mark

Bliss Isley worked for a time as a journalist and wrote several books.

moved to a Washington logging camp, where he was a lumberjack.

Not satisfied with his salary, Isley soon returned to Wichita and started work on The Wichita Beacon. In 1911, he started working for the Kansas City Star. He stayed there for a short time before moving on to the St. Louis Globe-Democrat and the Post-Dispatch.

But in 1918, Isely contracted tuberculosis and, in an effort to restore his health, moved back to the Wichita area. Once there, he handled publicity for the Federal Food Administration.

He wasn't on the job very long before he sustained a major lung hemorrhage that made him an invalid for several years.

When he retired at 74, he was writing a history series for Kansas Teacher, a section for Junior Encyclopedia, and for Scribner's Dictionary of American History and newspaper magazines. In 1958, the University of Wichita honored him for his contributions to American history.

Although Isely struggled with Parkinson's disease the last 10 years of his life, when not writing he devoted much of his time to growing broomcorn for friends and working on a 130-acre farm in the Flint Hills.

Isely died March 17, 1963. He

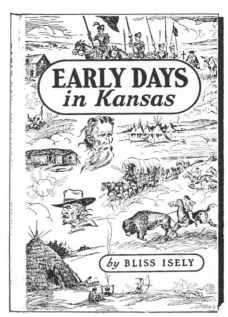

Bliss Isley wrote his first book, "Early Days in Kansas," in 1927. He wrote several others.

was 82.

"He was a very outgoing type," Ellington said. "He was very communicative with his writing and his personality. Even though his body was frail, the strength of the man was through his writing. To me, that's an outstanding accomplishment by itself."

on present-day historians," Ellington said. "They read his books and were inspired by Kansas' rich heritage. He conveyed history through a human-interest approach."

Isely was born Feb. 10, 1891, in Fairview. He graduated from Wichita's Fairmount College in 1906 and that year became a high school principal at Hamlin. In 1908, Isely

"Crazy Old Ed" Shutz

Decades later, a wrong has been righted

"To lose a friend in whom one had invested something of one's personality was, I discovered, to have lost a certain amount of one's self. The successful pursuit of the philosophy now before you demands that you restore whatever of your personality has been dissipated, carted off by other people. If any of its essential energy has been scattered, it must be recovered."
—Lloyd C. Douglas
"Doctor Hudson's Secret Journal"

It has taken almost seven decades since his death for "Crazy Old Ed" to be remembered. But now his grave bears a stone, paid for by a man who as a boy taunted him as he wandered the streets of Wichita.

It's a story of righting wrongs and bestowing respect; of an eccentric, lonely old man and a repentant neighborhood boy.

"Crazy Old Ed" was Ed Shutz, a junk dealer whom neighborhood children would spy on, run from and harass.

In 1924, Wichita was crawling with all sorts of modern activity. There were automobiles, streetcars, telephones and movie theaters.

But none of them was included in Shutz's life. He lived alone in the stone cottage he had built at 1416 E. Zimmerly.

Shutz was a hermit whose only visible pleasure came in the evenings when he would sit on his front porch and smoke a pipe.

Known as "Crazy Old Ed," Ed Shutz was a junk dealer who lived alone in this stone cottage at 1416 E. Zimmerly.

Each day he would faithfully hitch up his horse and wagon and drive through the neighborhoods, combing the back streets and alleys for junk he could sell.

And often running after him, calling him names, was a pack of neighborhood boys.

"We called him 'Crazy Old Ed' because he was a loner," said one of those boys, now a 73-year-old retired physician living in Fort Smith, Ark., who asked to remain anonymous. "He would go down the street, and we would taunt him."

The boys thought the dark-skinned and bearded man was odd—clinging to his old-time ways.

"We were afraid of him," the physician admitted.

The shame of that fear created an act of charity. The physician donated a headstone to be placed where Shutz was buried in 1924 in a pauper's grave in Highland Cemetery in northeast Wichita.

That year, on May 21, a car frightened Shutz's horse in the 200 block of South Clifton. When the wheels of his wagon struck the curb, Shutz was thrown to the pavement; his skull was fractured.

The Wichita City Undertaking Co. ambulance rushed him to St. Francis Hospital, but he died within 30 minutes of the accident, never regaining consciousness.

He was 72.

The Wichita Beacon said: "Mr. Shutz was a native of Switzerland, coming here about 1883. He had but one living relative in America, a brother who resides in California. . . . His living was made as a junk hauler and odd job worker. He was a recluse and had no close friends."

A misspelled headstone marked the pauper's grave at Highland Cemetery, where Ed Shutz is buried.

Few people attended Shutz's funeral, but one of the neighborhood boys was there—the one who is now a physician.

After the funeral, a stone misspelling Shutz's name and reading "Ed Schutz 1852-1924" was placed on the grave.

That could have been the end of Shutz's story.

But through the years, his memory has haunted that boy who wore overalls and ran barefoot in the summer and, along with everybody else, stole ice chips from the back of an ice wagon.

"I always felt bad," the physician said. "Here was the lonely old man that nobody liked, and he was buried in a pauper's grave. I have never known anyone to have been buried that way."

So in 1990, the doctor visited Wichita and found the grave.

"As I have become older, I have thought about that old man. Here was a man who could have told us stories about Switzerland. But we never gave him a chance."

The doctor wants people now to know that Shutz's life mattered. That's why he erected the stone in the summer of 1991.

The doctor is emphatic that his gift be anonymous. He recalls a story from a book published in the 1930s, "Doctor Hudson's Secret Journal." The premise is that the people you are associated with take pieces of your personality with them when they leave. In the book, a physician learns to help people secretly and, by so doing, discovers more about himself.

That is much what the Arkansas physician is doing now.

"When you see somebody in need, you help them," he said. "But you have to keep it a secret."

In May 1991, the physician contracted with Quiring Monument Co. to erect the $650 stone on Shutz's grave. It bears the inscription:

"Ed Shutz, born 1852 in Switzerland, died May 21, 1924, age 72. For the needy shall not always be forgotten, and the hope of the poor shall not perish forever. (Psalm 9:18)

"Erected by a friend in 1991."

Earl Browder

Communist's views were out of sync with his hometown

In his day, Earl Browder was one of Wichita's best-known native sons, a potent political voice and two-time presidential candidate.

But Browder was secretary of the U.S. Communist Party, a politician whose views were so out of sync with his hometown that he failed to win a single Wichita vote when he ran for president in 1936.

His house at 628 S. Fern, which stood in the way of highway development, was razed on Sept. 3, 1990.

Although his hometown shunned Browder when he ran for president in 1936, Browder's connection to his Wichita house was

The house where Earl Browder was born at 628 S. Fern. It was razed in 1990.

Dave Williams/The Wichita Eagle

Earl Browder "was quite powerful. The Communist Party was getting a foothold in the American scene. Earl Browder was a good orator and good communicator. He rose high in the ranks."

historically important.

"At the time, he was quite powerful," Ellington said. "The Communist Party was getting a foothold in the American scene. Earl Browder was a good orator and good communicator. He rose high in the ranks."

Browder, born in 1891, was a messenger for Western Union and worked for the Fourth National Bank and for C.E. Potts Drug Co.

At 16, he began studying the writings of Karl Marx. When he heard Socialist Eugene Debs speak in the Forum, the forerunner of Century II, he was so influenced that he began selling "Appeal to Reason," a large, popular Socialist newspaper, on local streets.

Browder left Wichita in 1911 and went to the Kansas City area. Active in the labor and Socialist movements, he went to jail rather than serve in the armed forces during World War I.

He helped organize the Communist Party in the United States in 1919, just after the Bolshevik Revolution in Russia.

After a 1927 trip to Asia, where he helped form the Chinese Communist Party, he was jailed again for traveling on a fraudulent passport. His Communist activities put him into jail for a third time, in 1940.

Browder became the party's national secretary in the early 1930s and held the job until 1945. Twice he was the Communist Party's presidential candidate against Franklin Roosevelt, getting 80,000 votes in 1936 and 47,000 in 1940.

But in 1945, Soviet dictator Joseph Stalin expelled him from the party, accusing him of "sowing dangerous opportunistic illusions" about the possibility of peaceful coexistence of the U.S. and Soviet social systems.

Browder died June 27, 1973, in Princeton, N.J., at 82.

"Durable" Del Crozier

Die-hard political candidate won attention but not elections

Although "Durable" Del Crozier dazzled crowds with his political style, he never won a race for office.

It wasn't for lack of trying. A 14-time loser, he ran for Sedgwick County sheriff seven times, City Commission four times, governor twice and Congress once. He also announced several times that he was available to be president of the United States.

Perhaps it was his style. At least two things made his campaigns different from those of other candidates. He dressed in an Uncle Sam costume and wore it to political gatherings. And he broadcast speeches from a loudspeaker on his car while driving the city's streets.

His slogans through the years were unusual, too:

1944 sheriff's election—"You'll know him by his whiskers."

1946 sheriff's election—"More and better whiskey for less money."

1968 presidential election—"I have the best platform: Stop the war!"

1972 congressional election—"Crozier for Congress. It pays $42,500. I want that job!"

Crozier came to Wichita from Michigan in 1917. He was 22 years old and had only a fifth-grade education. He worked several years for Chalmers Motor Car Co., which brought him to Wichita as a troubleshooter.

In 1920, he opened his own service station. In 1926, he became a service shop foreman for E.J. Rodda Chrysler Agency, and about a year later he leased a repair shop and parking garage at 220 S. Water. He also leased a parking lot at 240 N. Market from 1939 to 1945.

In October 1945, Crozier bought

Del Crozier dressed in an Uncle Sam costume during his campaigns, and he broadcast speeches from his car.

a 150-car parking lot at 207 S. Emporia. For years, it was the largest parking lot in Wichita.

But it was his passion for politics and his campaign style that made him memorable to many Kansans.

In 1968, then-Gov. Robert Docking wrote Crozier: "I am glad you are in good health and are hitting the campaign trail with all of your vigor and enthusiasm. Keep up the good work, and always maintain your interest in the elective process. The campaign wouldn't be the same without you."

But he wasn't always received in such good favor.

An article in the May 4, 1971, issue of The Wichita Beacon said: "Del Crozier claims his occupation

is sex, saving money and running for public office, was acquitted this morning in Municipal Court on a charge of improper use of a public address system."

Crozier, it seems, had been driving the streets broadcasting, "It's going to rain," and "Don't shovel snow or smoke, they are both man-killers."

During his court appearance, the article said, Crozier, then 76, asked the judge to read the ordinance aloud to him because he was hard of hearing.

"I'm an old man; I can't move very well, judge," he said. "The reason is because my underwear is too tight."

When local papers did political profiles of candidates, Crozier would always say he would be good for a political office because he was "just a damn smart business-man." He told reporters that he would cut out wild spending on taxes and promised everybody that they could drive a car and park it at Crozier Parking.

During a candidates' forum for the 1972 election for governor, Crozier refused to answer questions and instead played songs on his harmonica. He brought the crowd down with his rendition of "Red Wing" and his own political song.

Crozier was a fixture in town.

"He made the campaigns enjoyable," Ellington said. "My personal memory of him was his driving down the street in his car. If anything exemplified patriotism and getting people to vote, that would be Del Crozier. He enjoyed the excitement of a race."

Crozier died in March 1976 at age 81.

Beaches,
Bricks
and Flicks

"I felt pretty special working at the Miller (Theater). All the girls did who worked there. You see, back in the 1920s when the Miller first opened, they only picked the brightest and prettiest girls in Wichita to be usherettes. By the time 1953 rolled around that had pretty much worn off—but we still felt we were special anyway."
—Shirley George Towner

The Turner Opera House

Oysters were served at its grand opening

When singers such as Lillian Russell came to Wichita in the early 1880s, they generally headed to one entertainment hall to perform for local residents: the Turner Opera House at First and Market.

Although downtown Wichita also boasted Russell Hall, local historians say the Turner was by far the showcase spot, where Wichitans attended plays, operas, concerts and dances.

It was one of the first opera houses—the pride of Wichita. At the time, many of the people who made up the community were from the East Coast. They demanded culture.

The Turner was built by the Wichita chapter of the TurnVerein Society, an international organization that included most of the city's German residents. The society was organized in the early 19th century, when Napoleon was ruling Europe, as an exercise organization to prepare young men there for the resistance, said Bev Henline, a researcher on Wichita history.

The Wichita chapter was organized in the fall of 1871 and was considered the city's first health club. Local club members bought a small building at the southwest corner of First and Market for about $500, Ellington said. The building also housed several dances and entertainment programs. By 1879, with Wichita's population growing, the group felt the need for a larger, more elaborate structure.

So that year, the 25 members built the Turner Opera House on the same corner for $15,000.

The brick-and-stone structure had a stage, auditorium, parquet and balcony, and could seat 1,000 people.

It was an architectural wonder. The top had a cupola that was reminiscent of Thomas Jefferson's stylings, such as Monticello.

City records indicate that when the hall was opened on Nov. 7, 1879, the refreshments included

The Turner Opera House served as an entertainment center for Wichita for six years. Oysters and ice cream were among the refreshments when it opened.

oysters and ice cream.

"Oysters were very popular during the '70s and '80s," Henline said. "They were packed in ice and shipped by barrel."

During the years that the Turner Opera House was an entertainment center for Wichita's residents, local papers were filled with weekly and daily billings of upcoming events. On Feb. 13, 1886, for instance, The Wichita Eagle ran an advertisement billing "Uncle Tom's Cabin" as a "Mammoth Organization!! Great Company!! 25 people on stage with two imported trick donkeys."

The Turner quit operating as an opera house in 1886. Two years later, it was used as a city market and soon after was turned into a carriage company. From 1894 to 1899, the Peerless Steam Laundry occupied the building. Later, the building housed several commercial offices. The Turner building was razed in 1919 to make room for the Lassen Hotel.

The opera house building was razed in 1919 to make room for the Lassen Hotel.

Laura Rauch/The Wichita Eagle

Sandy Beach

It offered cool relief from the Kansas heat

For more than 40 years, Sandy Beach was a gathering spot for thousands of Wichitans seeking relief from hot Kansas summers.

It was the place for swim meets, Miss Kansas contests and Fourth of July celebrations.

It was a first-class bathing beach with nice soft sand. If residents of Wichita used their imagination, some said they could almost feel they were off the coast of the Pacific. It was always crowded and popular. It was a place to relax and enjoy the sun.

Norris Stauffer bought the property at 5800 S. Seneca in 1929 as a workout place for the wrestlers and boxers he promoted.

On that property, Stauffer had a goat farm that once supplied goat milk and yogurt to area athletes and children. The goats were later sold to the Mexican government to help replenish Mexican stocks during a famine in the 1940s.

Sandy Beach opened in 1930 and was known for its natural pure white sand and spring-fed pool. It was in that pool that Harold "Buddy" Siegel made exhibition dives from the beach's 152-foot, 6-inch tower, setting the water on fire with oil.

Another local celebrity, Fred McConnell, for whom the Air Force base was named, often frequented the beach to work out on gymnastics equipment.

At night, the beach would change its character. It was a wonderland of entertainment. There were different acts featured such as high-wire and musical entertainment. It just had a carnival atmosphere.

Along with the beach, there were shaded picnic areas, concession stands and a miniature golf course and bowling alley.

Stauffer was long associated with Wichita athletics for the first half of this century. He was director of the Elks Club activities, coached the city's first Amateur Athletic Union men's basketball team and helped organize and coach the Wallenstein & Rathman girls basketball team, which ranked as one of the country's best. Stauffer also promoted wrestling and boxing matches in Wichita. He died in 1959.

But the beach kept going until the 1970s, when it was closed.

"It was a neat little place," said Pat Utter, manager of Ginger's Boutique on South Seneca. "I just hated to see another one of our old places go."

Sandy Beach, which opened in 1930, was known for its natural pure white sand and spring-fed pool.

Dockum Drugstores

They boasted the finest soda fountains

Harry Dockum wasn't exactly a man about town, but his drugstores were.

Dockum Drug Co. was one of the major pharmacy chains in Wichita for more than 70 years.

He offered first-class drugstore service.

"The Dockum Drugstore fountains were pristine. They were the finest of soda fountains," Ellington said. "I can still taste the malts today. They were served with a cookie and a can half-filled with a malt. I can't tell you what those malts had in them, but I tell you they had a bit of heaven in them."

Dockum came to Wichita in 1899 and, along with Harry Higginson, started a drugstore on Jan. 1, 1900, at 248 N. Main. In 1903, their Dockum and Higginson Drugstore was joined by another store, the Palace Pharmacy, at 128 N. Main.

Later in the year, the partnership was dissolved with Higginson taking the store at 248 N. Main and Dockum the one at 128 N. Main. He named his store the Dockum Drug Co.

Harry Dockum operated drugstores.

A short time later, Dockum moved his store to 111 E. Douglas.

Dockum's first soda fountain was made from onyx, and above it was a latticework cupola enameled white. At that time, the city's electricity operated only at night. Dockum thought that he needed electric ceiling fans to keep his customers cool during the day, so when the public plant was shut down, he obtained an electric current from the street railway company, becoming the first store to have electricity during the day.

A newspaper article reported that the favorite drinks from the Dockum fountain were pingpong punch, sarsaparilla and sweet vanilla. There were also jumbo sodas and malts.

So successful was Dockum's first store that he and his son, Robert, eventually opened 12 more. The locations were 301 E. Douglas, 400 E. Douglas, 21st and Lawrence (now Broadway), Hillside and Douglas, Seneca and Douglas, 1557 S. Lawrence, 1400 N. Waco, 300 N. Main, Lincoln and Broadway, 4820 E. Douglas, 956 Parklane and 3901 S. Seneca.

When Dockum opened three downtown stores all within three blocks of one another, local papers later said some people doubted his business sense.

"It is said that he was foolish, that one store would take away trade from the other. But Dockum went ahead, and all three of the stores prospered," The Wichita Eagle reported on May 28, 1926. "The Dockum Drug company has kept pace with the times, and in each of the three stores is installed the latest and finest soda fountains."

For many, the Dockum stores were known as a place to meet. The environment was clean.

Every shelf, every item was always in place. Everything sparkled. And, it was always crowded. It was the in place to go with all walks of life and all ages.

Dockum was known for his "Harry Dockum Says" ads that sometimes offered bits of tongue-in-cheek philosophy and always promoted his stores.

"We are indeed very proud of our new offices and warehouse but we are not unmindful that it is our good friends and customers who have made these possible, and with this new equipment, we promise to give our patrons even better DOCKUM SERVICE than in the past," read one Harry Dockum Says ad in The Wichita Beacon on April 14, 1935.

Dockum died March 25, 1941. His last store closed in 1973. It was at 8903 W. Central.

Every shelf, every item was always in place in a Harry Dockum drugstore.

The Arkansas Valley Interurban

Electric trolly line linked three counties

The Arkansas Valley Interurban was the driving force behind a growing city's dream.

With a fleet of 11 Pullman passenger cars, the Interurban provided a daily rapid transit service from Wichita to Newton and on to Hutchinson for almost four decades.

This was what Wichita was hoping for in the ultimate of rural transportation. The AVI was a link to all satellite communities.

The idea for the Interurban

In Wichita, the Interurban depot was next to the Broadview Hotel at the northwest corner of Douglas and Waco. The depot was a two-story brick building.

started in 1903, when George Theis Jr., a Wichita capitalist, envisioned an electric trolley line that would connect five Kansas counties. The actual line connected only three—Sedgwick, Harvey and Reno—but was popular enough to carry nearly 1 million passengers a year.

The general manager of the Interurban was Robert Bruce Campbell, who later became known as Interurban Bob.

The Interurban began operation late in 1910, providing service between Wichita and Newton every two hours. By 1915 it had grown into a 63-mile track.

At the time, trains often took more than seven hours to travel between Wichita and Salina, with two to three layovers. AVI officials wanted to improve on that and proposed building a line from Wichita to Salina.

Although the track was never completed beyond Newton, the Interurban did deliver Wichita passengers to Hutchinson within two hours—a feat almost unheard of until the advent of automobiles.

The Interurban had terminals in Wichita, Newton and Hutchinson as well as station stops in Valley Center, Sedgwick, Van Arsdale, Halstead and Burrton.

In addition, there were shelter stops along the route.

In Wichita, the AVI depot was next to the Broadview Hotel, at the northwest corner of Douglas and Waco. The depot was a two-story brick building that contained a high-ceiling waiting room, an ornate ticket office and a large baggage room. A long foyer to Douglas Avenue was lined with small retail shops.

Wichita passengers could board the Interurban near where the Mid-America All-Indian Center stands today on Seneca, and at the golf course clubhouse in Sim Park, near today's Botanica. The Interurban also stopped near 13th Street and Perry, 17th and Garland, 19th and Woodland, and 21st and Mascot.

But by the 1920s, the AVI had lost much of its appeal, as more and more customers bought automobiles.

Thies was killed in an accident on Aug. 14, 1926. He died after being struck by a propeller of an airplane being taxied into an airport hangar.

Campbell became his successor, and the company struggled on. But during the Depression, the Interurban began to have financial problems and fell behind in taxes. Passenger service was discontinued in 1938. In 1939, H.E. Salzburg Co. of Chicago purchased the Interurban for $75,000.

By 1940, the trolley wires and substations had been removed. All

A map shows the route of the Arkansas Valley Interurban as well as a proposed line to Salina.

that remains of the Interurban is the freight passenger entrance on the Waco side of the Ramada Inn at Broadview Place, where the AVI initials are still visible. In some of the communities serviced by the Interurban, there still are cement arched trestles and evidence of the line's right of way.

In September 1991 the Great Plains Transportation Museum moved the depot from Sedgwick to its yards on East Douglas.

Ackerman Island

It lured first gold-seekers, then fun-seekers

Legend has it that in 1750, a group of Frenchmen navigated the Arkansas River in search of gold.

By sheer luck, they made their way to the river's source in the Rocky Mountains, where they came across a Spanish pack train loaded with gold. The French robbed the Spanish, loaded four boats filled with the gold and headed back down the river.

When they approached an island where the Arkansas River joins with the Little Arkansas, they stopped, made camp and cached the gold. That night, they were attacked by Indians, and only one man escaped to tell the story.

He never came back for the gold, but a 1757 French map of the Louisiana Territory shows a gold mine at the junction of the two rivers.

Old newspaper clippings say Jesse Chisholm came to the confluence of the Arkansas and Little Arkansas rivers in 1836, leading a group of men in search of the gold.

Older Wichitans might remember going to games in the ballpark on Ackerman Island. It was there until 1933, when a Works Progress Administration project funded the island's removal.

They never found it.

But the sandbars and islands near the confluence of the two rivers continued to draw the imaginations of the people who settled near them.

In 1890, the largest island became the property of Joseph Ackerman, a prominent businessman who came to Wichita in 1886 and operated a slaughterhouse and packing plant for four years until they were destroyed by fire. He lived on the island, where today's Second Street intersects the river, and operated a sand business there. The island belonged to the Ackerman family until 1905, when it was sold and became the site of an amusement park.

The park, known as Wonderland, featured the nation's longest roller coaster, a vaudeville theater, a swimming pool and a roller rink.

Wonderland was open until 1918, when blue laws prohibiting Sunday shows closed the theater, then the park's main attraction.

An aerial view of Ackerman Island, removed as a beautification project.

In 1919, the park was leased to The Palestinian Film Co. to be used as movie studios for a planned miniature "Hollywood." But when Wichita and the rest of the nation became involved in World War I, the movie project was canceled because of a shortage of local materials and men.

The Arkansas Valley Interurban, a local mass transit railroad system, was rerouted in 1921 to cross the island, and the barns that housed the cars were in the Wonderland section of the island.

Ackerman Island was used as a baseball park until 1933, when a federal Works Progress Administration project funded the removal of the island.

The island was removed as a beautification project, which narrowed the channel, put in McLean Boulevard and to some degree elevated some flooding concerns. But the primary concern was to get men back to work.

The project employed about 1,500 Wichita men who hauled dirt by wheelbarrow and tied the island to the river's west bank.

During its heyday, the island was about 3,500 feet long and 300 feet wide. By that time, it had been connected with other islands in the river.

When the island was removed the excitement of the area disappeared.

The Forum

Even Elvis was spotted at this popular auditorium

The Forum was a building that housed everything from 4-H stock shows, circuses, big-name entertainers and conventions to graduation exercises.

Even The King, Elvis Presley, made an appearance in the Forum when he was starting his career.

For years, Wichita's Forum was a place of popular assembly.

Shortly after the turn of the century, Wichita's leaders wanted a building that would be the equivalent of large auditoriums found in Chicago, New York, Denver or Kansas City. The Forum, on Water between William and English, was constructed in 1910 for $150,000.

The land the Forum stood on was considered prime. William Greiffenstein, the father of Wichita, built his homestead there. Finlay Ross, mayor of Wichita, in 1890 bought the Greiffenstein homestead for the city, paying $6,000.

Ross wanted the land for an open market where hay could be sold and farmers could display garden produce. For several years, his market flourished, but in 1909, the Legislature passed a law giving the city of Wichita power to vote bonds for an auditorium and market house.

The Forum opened on Jan. 25, 1911, with the show "Children's Crusade."

More than 700 adults and children performed, accompanied by the Cincinnati orchestra.

The general session of the 1931 convention of the Kansas State Teachers Association was held in the Forum, where 6,000 to 7,000 teachers gathered on alternate years.

One of the largest events in the Forum was the play "Ben Hur."

Newspaper accounts indicate that when the show was performed in 1911, dozens of people were in the cast. The scenery in "Ben Hur" was so detailed and elaborate that it required a treadmill so that 12 horses could stage a chariot race. And there were moving backgrounds to give the impression the horses were moving.

The crew members from the play's scenery company were so impressed with the new Forum that they fashioned a huge asbestos curtain advertising "Ben Hur." The curtain, complete with the seal of Kansas, was left behind when the show moved on, and it hung for years on stage. When the Forum was torn down in 1965, the curtains from the original show were donated to the Old Cowtown Historical Museum.

By 1917 an expansion was needed at the Forum and a second section was built. It included a market house and exposition hall for displaying livestock and agricul-

The Forum, on Water between William and English, was built in 1910 for $150,000. It was razed in 1965.

the Arcadia, was the city's largest ballroom. Both were in the north end of the Forum complex.

During World War II, the Forum housed military troops—including tanks as a patriotic effort to get local residents involved in the war effort.

The Forum was razed in 1965 and replaced with Century II.

The Forum was a place for contrasts.

"I remember going there and seeing wrestling matches," Ellington said. "I remember watching the adrenaline run through women's veins and hearing them scream and holler 'Kill him' during the height of the matches. Then, the next day going to the Forum again and listening to a fine and beautiful musical performance at the highest level of cultural entertainment."

tural products.

The Arcadia Theater building, next to the Forum, was constructed in 1917 to handle bookings that couldn't get into the Forum. The Rose Room, on the upper level near

The John Mack Bridge

"Rainbow" structure is one of a vanishing breed

From the day it was completed in 1930, the John Mack Bridge on South Broadway was hailed for its architectural beauty and cursed for its expensive, complex design. One of 70 bridges in Kansas designed by James Barney Marsh, it sported his hallmark rows of white, reinforced concrete arches.

But Marsh's "rainbow bridges" have become a vanishing breed, and the John Mack Bridge, with its 800-foot span across the Arkansas River, is one of the nation's largest survivors.

At one time there were more than 70 rainbow bridges in Kansas, said Larry Jochims, historian in the historic preservation department of the Kansas State Historical Society.

The John Mack Bridge on South Broadway is one of the rainbow bridges designed by James Barney Marsh.

Ken Mantyla/The Wichita Eagle

Now, he estimates, 30 are left.

Born in 1856 at North Lake, Wis., Marsh spent the early part of his career designing, selling and erecting metal bridges. In the spring of 1896, he formed the Marsh Bridge Co.

At the turn of the century, he had pioneered the use of concrete and steel spans in his bridge designs. His rainbow arch proved to be a big hit for major stream crossings in Kansas.

"That type of bridge was very popular in the late 1920s and 1930s," Jochims said. "Contractors hated the bridges because they were so expensive and detailed to build. But they were very popular with the general public.

"People saw them as beautiful and monumental."

Wichita's rainbow arch bridge was named after Highway Commissioner John Mack, then editor of the Newton Journal, who negoti-

ated the final contract for the bridge from his deathbed. The bridge replaced an iron bridge.

Shortly after the bridge was built, South Lawrence Avenue, then a two-lane street, was widened to four lanes and renamed Broadway.

Portions of old Lawrence Avenue, a brick road, still border Watson Park on the east.

Through the years, the bridge has been a local landmark and a favorite of children.

Train depots

Early railways shipped cattle, tripped up motorists

When trains began rolling into Wichita in 1872, city leaders were quick to seize the new industry and merge it with their own commercial interests.

The city's first railroad was the Wichita and Southwestern Railway Co., which later became the Santa Fe. Its depot was where the north end of the Douglas Avenue overpass stands today.

The early trains were used primarily to ship cattle from this area.

About the time the trains started arriving, Wichita's milling businesses started to expand, and that created a demand for additional railroad facilities.

The depot the Rock Island used in 1909 still stands, but today it is home to Prudential-Bache Securities rather than railroad passengers.

The Frisco depot occupied land where The Wichita Eagle now stands, on Douglas at Rock Island.

Commerce was being developed. The increased rail traffic brought in not only passengers but an increase in imported goods.

The Frisco line—the St. Louis-San Francisco Railroad—came to Wichita in 1879, followed three years later by the St. Louis, Fort Scott and Wichita, which later became the Missouri Pacific. Also that same year, the Wichita and Western arrived in the city.

"We were starting to be a hub," Ellington said. "Then, the Kansas Midland was developed. After that, the Rock Island came in 1887.

"Maps were published showing all these railroads feeding into this town. It looked like a great city in the making."

By the turn of the century, most Kansas towns had one or two railroads through their city limits. Wichita had five major railroads.

But with the growth came hardships. Travel on Douglas from the Arkansas River east was almost impossible during certain times of the day.

That much rail traffic, combined with automobile and horse and buggy traffic, created huge traffic jams.

The horse and buggy drivers found it quite an exasperating experience. Horses would get shaken up by the noise from passenger and freight trains, Ellington said.

In 1909, three depots stood in a one-block area on Douglas. There was the Rock Island, which still stands, as Prudential-Bache Securities at 711 E. Douglas; the Santa Fe, where Multimedia Cablevision is housed, at 701 E. Douglas; and the Frisco, where The Wichita Eagle is, at 825 E. Douglas.

That year, Charles Davidson ran a successful campaign for mayor by promising to start negotiations between the city and the railroads to see whether an overpass could be built that would allow trains to pass over Douglas and traffic to pass underneath.

In 1910 the three railroads agreed to elevate their tracks from Kellogg past Second Street and construct an impressive station.

Construction started in 1913, and the project was completed a year later.

The result was Union Station.

For a city of Wichita's size, residents considered themselves lucky to have such an impressive station. It meant improved pedestrian traffic. It improved the safety conditions because the passing of the many trains posed a danger to not only pedestrians but also to those

The Santa Fe depot was on the spot that became Wichita's Union Station, which today houses Multimedia Cablevision.

Union Station was the result of an agreement between three railroads.

in buggies and primitive motor vehicles. It was a significant undertaking and encouraged others to come to Wichita.

Visitors spread the word.

But by the 1960s, when the popularity of air traffic had increased, Wichita's passenger service was beginning to wane. And on Oct. 6, 1979, the last passenger train, Train No. 16 of the Lone Star Amtrak, left Wichita.

The Miller Theater

Moviegoers dressed up to attend this cinema showcase

In 1953, Shirley George Towner was 16 years old and working as an usherette in the Miller Theater.

She recalled it was a heady, exhilarating experience. She originally worked at the Palace Theater and went to the Miller to work when the Palace was sold.

"I felt pretty special working at the Miller," she said. "All the girls did who worked there. You see, back in the 1920s when the Miller first opened, they only picked the brightest and prettiest girls in Wichita to be usherettes. By the time 1953 rolled around that had pretty much worn off—but we still felt we were special anyway."

Beginning May 1, 1922, the Miller Theater showcased almost 50 years of Wichita's finest entertainment. On opening night, more than 10,000 people came to see the movie "Beyond the Rocks" with Gloria Swanson and Rudolph Valentino. Eight thousand of them had to be turned away from the 2,000-seat theater. Those who got in paid 25 cents or 35 cents to see the movie.

The Miller also first presented talking movies in Wichita. The very first, "When a Man Loves" with John Barrymore, opened May 13, 1928.

Towner, who lives in Salina, described the Miller as "palatial."

And indeed it was. The building material included $25,000 worth of marble from France, 2,000 yards of Wilton carpet, $4,500 worth of

With marble floors and plush carpeting, the Miller Theater in its heyday was one of the nicest around.

glass, 400,000 bricks and 150,000 pieces of tile and terra cotta. Total cost of construction was more than $750,000.

The Miller, at 115 N. Broadway, was the type of theater that people dressed up to go to. A uniformed, white-gloved footman stood in front to help people out of their cars, and the theater had 30 ushers and usherettes to help patrons find seats.

"Back in those days the theaters were crowded," Towner said. "Very often people couldn't find seats. An usherette walked the crowd. She knew where there were vacant seats. And if a couple came up and asked for two seats together, she would see they would get the seats they wanted."

The Miller also was known as a place where people could escape Kansas' weather. The Wichita Eagle predicted on April 30, 1922, that the Miller would be known as having the coolest temperatures in the city during summer months.

"This fact is due to the installation of two ventilating systems, either of which is capable of providing proper ventilation.

"When architects presented the plans of the theater to L.M. Miller, owner of the new show house, they showed him one ventilating system, which was guaranteed to keep the building at the proper temperature. Mr. Miller said that this was in nine cases out of 10 true, but that he knew Kansas weather and wanted the coolest theater in the city in hot weather, so instructed

When designing the Miller Theater, the owner had two ventilating systems installed to make sure it was the coolest theater in town during Wichita's hot summer months.

the plans be altered to provide for another ventilating system."

The Miller was named after Lewis Miller, a dentist from Lincoln, Neb. He was born in Washington Court House, Ohio, in 1876 and graduated from Northwestern University in Chicago. In 1901 he went into partnership with a brother and began operating theaters in Lincoln.

He moved to Wichita in 1909 and built the Princess Theater at 121 S. Broadway, later the site of Innes, Macy's and Dillards department stores, and the Palace Theater at 309 E. Douglas, later the site of Brick's Men's Wear.

He opened the Miller as a showcase.

In addition to films, the Miller also ran live stage shows and featured appearances by celebrities. Will Rogers was a big drawing card. So was Charlie Chaplin, who appeared there several times. There also were evening music programs on Wednesdays, featuring the 20-

Lewis Miller was a dentist from Lincoln, Neb.

piece Miller Orchestra and the theater's Wurlitzer organ.

"The Miller was a movie theater of the real movie theater genre," Towner said.

The Miller closed in 1970, partly because the number of people attending movies was dwindling and movie theaters were springing up in other parts of the city, such as in the Twin Lakes Shopping Center. The last movie shown was "Safety Last," a silent film. The building was razed in 1972 to make room for the Fourth National Bank parking lot.

"They tore down the theaters to make way for office buildings and parking lots, and now there is nothing left in downtown Wichita for people," Towner said. "The last time I went to the Miller was in 1966. I took my girls to see a movie. We walked down to Douglas to catch a bus; it was only 6 in the evening. Everything was dead. There weren't any lights. There weren't any people. The theaters were a big part of downtown life."

The Orpheum Theater

A city within a city, it created that magic feeling

When it opened Labor Day weekend in 1922, Wichita's Orpheum Theater was considered a city within a city.

With its adjoining seven-story office building, the Orpheum, at First and Broadway, housed several shops and businesses. It attracted doctors, lawyers and barbers. But more important, the theater was a showplace that promised to transport its drama and movie patrons to more exotic locales.

The walls of the theater were painted with scenes that depicted "beautiful peacocks and pigeons perched on the roof of the Spanish boxes on the side walls near the stage," said George Graves, who recalled the opening for the Sept. 1, 1960, Wichita Eagle. "Looking above into the blue heavens, we could see the stars twinkling, and it gave you the feeling you could be on the patio in some Spanish villa."

Even so, the gala opening was

The Orpheum Theater, in keeping with the latest in the motion picture industry, was wired for sound in 1929. Its last movie was shown in 1976.

The Orpheum's first show included five vaudeville acts. Its curtains opened 17,000 times over the years.

somewhat marred.

Air conditioning was nonexistent, Kansas temperatures were soaring, and the Orpheum's audience was sweating on the red leather seats. When the dye from the seats bled onto the patrons' clothes, tempers flared. That's when the management promised to pay the cost of cleaning everyone's clothes. The cleaning bill? More than $1,800 for that first showing.

"The management scurried around to get covers for the seats before the evening show, and the red seats remained covered until they were replaced or re-covered," Graves said in the 1960 interview. The solution was white canvas covers purchased from Ponca Canvas Products Co.

The theater's first show included an organ recital, feature pictures and five vaudeville acts.

The Orpheum was designed by one of the nation's leading theater architects, "Opera House John" Eberson. He designed more than 100 theaters across the nation. His trademark was the depiction of atmospheric scenes from nature through the use of gazebos, trellises, columns, arches, chandeliers and vaulted ceilings. His theaters featured ceilings with clouds and handfuls of low-wattage stars.

Eberson's slogan was "Prepare Practical Plans for Pretty Playhouses Please Patrons Pay Profits"

It was as if the outdoors were suddenly brought indoors.

"It was the ultimate gathering place and had a festive flavor about it," Ellington said. "It was generally packed all the time. I remember that it had perfect acoustics. You could stand in the last row of the balcony and hear the voices from the stage without any amplification at all."

The Orpheum operated until 1929 mostly as a vaudeville house, although some short feature pictures were shown.

An Eagle clipping of Sept. 3, 1922, said, "Only young men who are working their way through school or college are to be em-ployed as ushers in the theater. All ushers are to wear handsome suits of Spanish influence and colorings." Their costumes were lavender jackets with black flowing pants, red sash and a black fedora-style hat.

In 1929, in keeping with the latest developments in the motion picture industry, the 1,700-seat auditorium was wired for sound.

All told, there were 17,000 performances in the Orpheum. Crowds came to see Jack Benny, Gypsy Rose Lee, Harry Houdini and members of Our Gang.

Because of parking problems and downtown congestion, crowds began to dwindle during the late 1960s and early 1970s. In 1976, the last regular Hollywood movie ran through the Orpheum's projector. For a short time, Spanish language and X-rated movies were shown. The last movie shown was on martial arts. The theater was closed later that year.

The Orpheum's office tower was closed in the 1960s, said Dave Burk, an architect whose office, Breidenthal & Burk, is in the building. The office tower was restored and reopened in 1984.

The Orpheum was nominated for local landmark status on June 28, 1978, and in February 1979 the Wichita City Commission designated the building and the theater's interior as a historic landmark. Two years later, the building was entered in the National Register of Historic Places.

"It's our last remaining grand theater in our downtown area," Burk said. "It is a part of our historic fabric. I would like to see it eventually renovated."

Posted on the Orpheum's switchboard backstage was this notice to all stage personnel, perhaps explaining the Orpheum's magic while it lasted:

"Please do not turn on the clouds until the show starts. Be sure the stars are turned off when leaving."

Hot Air,
Schemes
and Scandals

*"He set out to make Wichita Kansas'
largest city. He and the group of men
who built Wichita came here to build a
city, not just another Kansas town.
They willed it to be. They created with
words what gold and silver created in
the Black Hills and Colorado. They
created a land boom based on nothing
but their hot air."*
—*Stan Harder, curator of Old Cowtown
Museum, on William Greiffenstein,
co-founder of Wichita*

William Greiffenstein

His "hot air" sent Wichita soaring

If William Greiffenstein were to walk down Douglas Avenue today, chances are he would be very pleased.

"He set out to make Wichita Kansas' largest city," said Stan Harder, curator of Old Cowtown Museum. "He and the group of men who built Wichita came here to build a city, not just another Kansas town. They willed it to be. They created with words what gold and silver created in the Black Hills and Colorado. They created a land boom based on nothing but their hot air."

Greiffenstein, an enterprising trader from Germany, came to the Wichita area in 1867. Local historians credit him as being Wichita's father because in 1871, he planned Wichita's business district along Douglas Avenue.

But even before then, he had carved out a name as a leader.

As early as 1850, Greiffenstein had started a trading business with

Trader William Greiffenstein helped build downtown Wichita.

the Shawnee and Delaware Indians on a reservation six miles east of Lawrence.

"His trading route ran from New Mexico to Topeka," Harder said. "He established himself as a trader among the Cheyenne, Arapaho, Kiowa, Comanche and Apache."

In 1867, Greiffenstein built a trading post along the Cowskin Creek, where Wichita is now. Other traders, such as Jesse Chisholm and Elias Hicks Durfee, also were locating in the area by then.

"There wasn't anything to lure him," Harder said. "He came here before the city. If anything lured him, it was the lucrative trade between the wants of the white folks for furs and the wants of the Indians. As a middleman, he made a lot of money."

By 1868, Greiffenstein and Wichita businessman Darius Munger began platting Wichita's streets, Harder said. Munger platted Waco near Ninth Street, and Greiffenstein platted along Main near First and Second streets.

As more people began to settle in

William Greiffenstein constructed two major buildings near where Century II is today.

The Douglas Avenue House was one of the first buildings on Douglas Avenue. Some early Wichitans thought William Greiffenstein was foolish to develop Douglas.

the community, businesses sprang up on Main Street.

But in 1872, Greiffenstein flabbergasted some of the residents by constructing two major buildings—the Eagle Block Building and the Douglas Avenue House—in what was then the middle of nowhere, Douglas Avenue. The buildings were near where the Finlay Ross Park and Century II are today at Douglas and Water, Harder said.

"He pulled a switcheroo on the group who bought into the lots on Main Street," Harder said. "I can imagine the group on the north end of Main Street started watching the elaborate buildings going up. At first, they thought Greiffenstein was a fool, having his buildings face away from Main Street. Then they started getting angry."

Greiffenstein was looking to make money, Harder said, and he had the foresight to see that people would pay money to locate businesses on the stretch of land running east from the Arkansas River to the railroad. The railroad remains there today.

An article from the Sept. 18, 1909, Wichita Eagle reported that to make his land more valuable, Greiffenstein took the majority of stock in the old toll bridge and secured its location at Douglas Avenue. The toll bridge is where the Douglas Bridge stands today.

"Then, he took stock and became a director in the company which built the first railway into Wichita, connecting with the Santa Fe (Railway). With the power of his directorship, he secured the location of the freight depot at Douglas Avenue," the newspaper said.

With the bridge at the west end of the street and the railroad and depot at the east, traffic was forced along Douglas, and businesses followed.

"The end result was that the major commercial downtown development area became Douglas rather than Main Street," Harder said. "Even after the herding of Texas cattle stopped in 1876, and when the agrarian community came to Wichita, people would naturally go down Douglas to do their shopping. And so, Douglas became the commercial center for this part of the country. It still is today."

On March 25, 1910, The Eagle reported that 40 years earlier on that day, "The first plat of the town was made on a grocery bag; large size, and split open as we had nothing else. It is in the recorder's office in Wichita at the courthouse."

Greiffenstein served as Wichita's mayor from 1878 to 1884.

He died in Indian Territory where he had hopes of developing a new town in the 1890s.

Greiffenstein and his wife, Catherine, are buried in Wichita's Highland Cemetery.

Marshall Murdock

The need for a newspaper lured him to town

The year Marshall Murdock stepped into town, Wichita was just a baby.

A cord of wood cost $5, wooden sidewalks lined Main Street, and the railroad had started to wind its way into town.

It was 1872. Wichita promoters were luring the 35-year-old Murdock to town from Burlingame. They wanted a strong paper for the community, and he wanted to operate a newspaper.

The railroad held the promise of the town becoming a shipping point. In many ways, the railroad was the turning point for Wichita's economy. Before that, Wichita was just a stop on the Chisholm Trail.

Once it had been established that Wichita would indeed have a railroad, town leaders such as James R. Mead and William Greiffenstein asked Murdock to come. They

Marshall Murdock wanted to name his newspaper The Victor. His wife objected.

promised him that Wichita would be a progressive community—a quality that appealed to Murdock.

"The Wichita people who had some investment in this community knew of Murdock's reputation both as a newspaperman and his political abilities," Ellington said. "The town had experienced two newspapers before that, but the promoters knew they needed a first-class journal to promote their town. He was asked and he accepted."

Murdock was born in Morgantown, W. Va., on Oct. 10, 1837. His father, Thomas, moved the family to Lawrence in the 1850s. When gold was found in Colorado, Murdock traveled to Leadville, where he is credited with finding the first silver in the area.

While he was searching for gold, the Civil War broke out and he came back to Kansas to care for the younger members of the family. His two oldest brothers and his father left to join the Union forces.

By the time the war was over, Murdock had not only become the editor of the Burlingame Chronicle but also had served as a state senator from Osage and Coffey counties and escaped William Quantrill and his raiders by hiding in the lower portion of a privy.

But Murdock was feeling restless with eastern Kansas and beginning to realize that Burlingame was not going to become a city. He liked the growth taking place in Wichita and decided to move.

Wichita was ready for him because there was news to report.

"We feel confident that we are becoming identified with a liberal, good and home-loving people,"

Murdock wrote in the first issue of The Wichita Eagle on April 12, 1872. "To print a paper worthy of such a community's support, a paper that will be welcomed by every family and place of business in the city and by every fireside and homestead in the valley, is now our highest ambition and will be our studied duty."

Murdock was going to name the new paper The Victor in honor of his wife, Victoria. But she thought the name inappropriate and favored The Eagle because the bird was the symbol of American freedom and liberty. They decided to flip a coin to settle the question. She called tails and won.

Besides his role as a journalist, Murdock served as postmaster of Wichita from 1874 to 1886 and from 1898 to 1908.

He died on Jan. 2, 1908.

"Being an editor and publisher of a newspaper gave him some prestige," Ellington said. "I think he was looked upon with a certain amount of awe. He did have that respect. His wife also was well-respected. They were always ones who were entertaining guests—important people from all over the state of Kansas."

Garfield University

Forerunner of Friends University had a short life

During the 1880s, while some promoters were building railroads, factories and office buildings, other Kansans joined to make Wichita an educational center.

Garfield University was the result.

Named for President James A. Garfield, the building erected in 1886 on the west edge of the city was the largest university in the state at the time. For some promoters, it was to be the gateway of higher education in the Southwest.

The school was built during the height of Wichita's boom. The investors were promoting lot additions near the school in addition to the school itself. The idea was to give the residential section more prestige.

The project began in 1885 when the Christian Church (Disciples of Christ) of Kansas voted to establish the university. The original site was at 2100 University, the homestead of R.E. Lawrence, a well-known developer in Wichita and one of the men after whom Lawrence-Dumont Stadium was named. Lawrence sold 120 acres of his homestead for $12,000.

In July 1886, work began. The main building was to be an elaborate structure, covering nearly three-fourths of an acre. And although not all the construction work had been completed—the front steps had not been built—the university doors were opened to 735 students about a year later. The curriculum included theology, music, law, medicine, business and fine arts.

By 1888, university records reported, there were 1,070 students.

Garfield University was a success in terms of attendance, but the lots surrounding the university failed to sell. And by 1892, when Kansas had had two years of crop failure, school officials could no longer afford to keep Garfield open.

James Davis bought the defunct Garfield University for $50,000.

What became Davis Hall was the only building left standing when James Davis bought Garfield University and donated it to the Kansas Yearly Meeting of the Society of Friends. Friends University began as Garfield University in 1887.

The doors were nailed shut and the windows boarded up. For more than six years, the building sat vacant. Owls, sparrows and bats were its only occupants.

Finally James Davis, a wealthy investor from St. Louis, noticed a full-page newspaper advertisement about a defunct university in Wichita. The ad promised that the university building could be purchased cheaply.

Davis came to Wichita, walked to the empty Garfield University, tore a board from the window, crawled through and inspected the building.

He bought the university and the surrounding lots for $50,000. He signed the deed in March 1898 and offered the university to the Kansas Yearly Meeting of the Society of Friends, with the stipulation that $50,000 in endowment funds be raised by 1904.

The university was renamed Friends University. And the only building standing at that time, the one Davis saved, was later renamed Davis Hall in his honor.

The Alumni Auditorium was finished in 1925 and the Fellow-Reeve Museum was opened in 1929. Both are in Davis Hall.

Other buildings on the Friends University campus include the president's home, constructed in 1910.

There also are Sumpter Hall, the college of business, built in 1950; Fry Hall, the women's dormitory, 1958; Woolman Hall, the men's dormitory, 1958; and the Whittier Fine Arts Center, constructed in 1965. The Edmund Stanley Library was built in 1970; the Garvey building, which houses the gymnasium, the art department and a radio

tion, was built in 1970. The William Penn Hall Science Building was constructed in 1973. The Casado Campus center was completed in 1989. And the Friends Village, a retirement complex, was built in 1985.

"It's a miracle that it was saved," Ellington said. "Had it not been for the gentleman from St. Louis, we probably would not have had Friends University. The building would have been razed."

In 1971, Davis Hall was placed on the National Register of Historic Places.

David Payne

Adventurer was a pain to federal officials

David Payne almost always received mixed reviews.

To his friends, he was an unsung hero—an adventurer who tried to settle untamed lands. To some federal government officials, he was a thorn in the backside who threatened to break Indian treaties.

During the 1880s, Payne made a habit of claiming unassigned lands in Indian Territory, which later was to become the state of Oklahoma. He argued that because the lands were unoccupied, they were subject to the Homestead Act. The federal government disagreed.

Time and time again, Payne and his band of "boomers" would invade Indian Territory. Time and time again, federal troops would drive them back to Kansas.

And it wasn't until five years after his death in 1884 that Payne's cause won out and he became known as "The Father of Oklahoma."

Payne was born in Indiana in 1836. His mother was a first cousin of Davy Crockett.

Payne served with the Union Army for three years during the Civil War. In 1864, he was elected to the Kansas Legislature. He later became its sergeant at arms.

In 1870, he arrived in Wichita and started a ranch in northeast Sedgwick County, where Payne Township is now. He built a small

David Payne led 132 wagons, 553 men and three women into Indian Terrority in 1883. He was arrested, as he was the next year when he led 1,500 settlers into the Cherokee Strip.

shack, a horse corral and a shed. Payne's Ranch, on the road between Towanda and Wichita, became a stopping place for travelers.

"In Wichita, he was very well liked," Ellington said. "He had some setbacks and lost his land through bad business deals. But he was well enough liked and respected for the people to name a township after him."

By the early 1880s, Payne had begun organizing his bands of "boomers."

They first invaded Indian Territory on Feb. 1, 1883. Payne left Arkansas City with 132 wagons, 553 men and three women. They made camp at the present site of Oklahoma City but were immediately driven out by federal troops.

Payne and three other men were walked to nearby Fort Reno and jailed for nine days.

The next spring, Payne took 1,500 settlers into the Cherokee Strip about four miles south of Hunnewell. Again the troops came, and Payne was put in irons and taken to Fort Smith, Ark., for trial. He later was released.

Opportunity always presented itself out on the prairies. People in Wichita and surrounding areas saw the Oklahoma lands as opportunity.

On Nov. 28, 1884, Payne died and was buried in Wellington. Nearly 5,000 people attended his funeral.

His death added fuel to a fiery debate.

Largely because of pressures from the movement Payne started, the federal government opened Indian Territory to settlement beginning in 1889.

The Wichita Watch Factory

It was the wrong time for the new industry

In the summer of 1889, the hopes and dreams of Wichita businessmen vanished when the Wichita Watch Factory failed.

The factory, on what is now the northeast corner of Douglas and Meridian, was to have built watches rivaling those made by Elgin and other watch companies.

But in 1889, before a single watch was built, those dreams were

crushed when Wichita's land and investments market fell.

"It was near completion," Ellington said of the factory. "They had actually started the machinery and had started seeking the watchmakers. It was fully operational. The watches were even going to have the Wichita logo on it. They just didn't have the money to operate."

Two years earlier, more than a dozen Wichita men gathered to discuss the watch company and the industrial potential for the city.

On July 17, 1887, The Wichita City Eagle reported: "The Peabody watch can be manufactured as cheaply, that is at a bigger profit and at as low a price, as that of any other standard watch manufactured by the Elgin, United States, Ameri-

A wing of the Wichita Watch Factory was completed in late 1887, and the factory was ready for business in the summer of 1889.

can or Waltham watch companies, and if the proper interest can be aroused, Mr. (Roswell) Peabody has signified his willingness, his desire in fact, to locate in Wichita over any city or town that he has yet visited."

Wichitans invested in the watch company, and the local architectural firm of Proudfoot and Bird began plans for a factory building. The six-acre factory site was on Chicago Avenue, which later became West Douglas.

The Eagle reported on Aug. 10, 1887, that one wing of the plant would be constructed by fall. It would be a stone structure, three stories high, with a machine shop, an engine house, a dial shop and a storehouse. The factory, in full operation, was to employ 400 people.

"While the business management of the company is disposed to be conservative and careful, nothing will be left undone to make the watch factory the foremost enterprise of Wichita; one that will be an ornament to the locality, a profit to the stockholders and a source of pride to the city. The company's directory is sufficient guarantee of its good faith," the paper promised supporters.

Work was proceeding and hopes were high because at the time, Wichita's real estate market was ranked third in the nation in volume of sales and turnovers. New York City was first and Kansas City second.

Throughout the city, people were promoting land and investments. And one of the largest investments was in the watch factory.

"The watch factory was a hope for additional commerce and industry on the west side," Ellington said. "But when the bust occurred, it left one of the largest vacancies of a fallen industry."

City co-founder William Greiffenstein was one of the hardest hit by the bust. It was enough to wipe him out. He tried to put his home up for sale. Finally, discouraged, he left Wichita for Oklahoma and had hopes of starting another Wichita in Oklahoma.

As the years went by, the steam engine from the factory was sold to an irrigation company. The shell of the old stone building sat vacant until 1903, when it was torn down by parishioners and used in St. Mark's Catholic Church.

The property now has houses and a few businesses such as Guaranteed Foods Inc. and Cole's Show Case.

"The building stood for nearly a decade, a haven for owls and birds," Ellington said. "There wasn't a thing in it. They didn't have an adaptive use for it. It was tight times for Wichita because we were going through a recession."

Guaranteed Foods Inc. and Cole's Show Case now occupy part of the site of the Wichita Watch Factory.

Dave Williams/The Wichita Eagle

Debt was his legacy; scandal marked his exit

For 11 years, Scott Winne was one of Wichita's Golden Boys.

From 1897 until 1908, Winne was the epitome of success. He established the Winne Mortgage Co., the Land Credit Trust Co. and the Land Credit State Bank. His chief stock-in-trade was selling Land Credit bonds, which drew interest at 5 percent. He lived in a mansion, at 10th and Jefferson, built by town founder William Greiffenstein; owned the Winne building; and supported charities about town.

But in late March 1908, Winne disappeared with $300,000 that many believe was money acquired through investors.

It was a shock to the community, mainly because the man was such a prominent fixture. There wasn't much people could do.

Originally from Hutchinson, Winne came to Wichita in 1897. At that time, he was considered an authority on Kafir-Corn, a drought-resistant corn that promised high yields. An 1896 brochure distributed by the Kansas Immigration and Information Association and written by Winne touted the crop and helped establish Winne's name

Scott Winne was never heard from again after he left Wichita.

The building at 210-212 E. Douglas was constructed in 1887-88 by Mike Zimmerly.

throughout the state.

Not long after his arrival in Wichita, Winne's interests moved to land investments. During the early part of the century, Winne bought the Zimmerly Building, one of the larger business structures in the community.

The building at 210-212 E. Douglas was constructed in 1887-88 by Mike Zimmerly. When Zimmerly lost the mortgage, Winne purchased the foreclosed property for $35,000 and renamed it. The building was a Wichita landmark until it was razed in 1956 for construction of the Lerner Store.

Winne's disappearance caused one of the biggest scandals in Wichita's history. A March 31, 1908, article in the Wichita Daily Beacon said Winne was hard up for cash.

"Just before leaving he canceled the insurance on his home, and took cash rebates for unearned premiums. These amounted to $178. That Winne should be willing to leave all this property unprotected for a paltry sum of $178 leads to the conclusion that he was hard pressed."

As the days and weeks passed, townspeople discovered that Winne had left with more than $178. He left huge debts. A July 15 headline of The Wichita Eagle said "Winne Indebtedness May Reach $700,000."

A lawsuit was settled in 1909,

The Lerner Building was built in 1956 on the site of the old Zimmerly Building, a Wichita landmark, which Scott Winne purchased from the original builder.

Gregory Drezdzon/The Wichita Eagle

when the Land Credit directors were able to produce $100,000 for partial repayment to bondholders. Judge T.C. Wilson, who ruled on much of the proceedings in District Court, set recovery rate at 42 percent; each $100 bond paid $42.

Winne was never heard from again, although occasionally some Wichita residents claimed they saw him in New York, then in Uruguay, Australia, Detroit and other places.

Ellington said Winne's descendants later told him that Winne went to Pittsburgh, Pa., and that he was eventually buried in a potter's grave near San Francisco.

Lorenzo Lewelling

His term as governor started with a legislative showdown

In the winter of 1893, after Lorenzo Lewelling was inaugurated as the state's 12th governor, angry words and fists flew in the Kansas House of Representatives.

It was a showdown between the Republicans and the People's Party, also known as the Populists, for control of the state Legislature.

For Lewelling, a Populist and the first Wichitan to become governor, the legislative war of 1893 was a chance to show that his party could play a vital role in Kansas politics. And it was a chance to show his power as governor. So, to establish order in the House, he called in 250 militiamen from across the state.

The incident became known as the Lewelling War.

At that time, the Populist Party was a strong political body with new ideas. The problem with the Lewelling War was that it went on for quite a few days. It was an emo-

Lorenzo Lewelling was a Populist.

tionally charged time—at times, dangerous.

The beginnings of the Lewelling

War actually came the year before, when Wichita served as the meeting place for the state convention of the Populist Party. The convention was in Wichita's auditorium, on the southwest corner of First and St. Francis.

Lewelling welcomed the convention-goers with a speech so impassioned that he was selected the party's nominee for governor. Later that year, as the Populist Party's momentum grew, the Democratic Party swung its support in favor of the Populists. The party controlled a majority in the Senate and about half of the 125-member House.

The papers made great news of it.

In many ways, it was ironic that Lewelling fueled such a volatile situation. He was born in 1846 near Salem, Iowa. His father was a Quaker minister. Both his parents had died by the time he was 9 years old, so Lewelling lived for a short time with a married sister.

When the Civil War broke out, he enlisted in an Iowa regiment. But fighting was against the family's religion, and his relatives secured his discharge.

His family's decision was not necessarily Lewelling's choice.

Lewelling then joined a bridge-building corps in Chattanooga, Tenn., and earned enough money to enter Eastman's Business College in Poughkeepsie, N.Y. After graduation, he returned to Salem, where he attended Whittier College. Lewelling came to Wichita in 1887 and established a small produce company on East Douglas.

"He was a very compassionate

The militia and a battery of Gatling guns turned the state grounds into a battleground. The conflict was finally resolved by the state Supreme Court.

man," Ellington said. "Money was not an object in his life. He gave much of himself to others, financially and otherwise. He did whatever deeds he could to help people out."

On Jan. 10, 1893, the first day of the Legislative session in Lewelling's term, the House of Representatives turned to chaos. Both the Republican and Populist parties were determined to be the majority party, so each elected its own speaker and tried to bring the House to order. Neither party was willing to recognize the powers of the other.

That action split the House.

Stubbornness set in, and the politicians remained in their chairs for several days. Each side was afraid to adjourn. Each side allowed tensions to build.

Finally, by February, tensions had risen to the point that Lewelling called in the militia and a battery of Gatling guns.

On Valentine's Day, the Republicans tried to arrest Ben Rich, the Populist chief clerk, who, they said, had "continually interrupted the House by loud and boisterous language and unlawful and unusual noises."

Both sides began swearing at sergeants at arms.

Soon, the state grounds began to resemble a battleground, with sentries posted, soldiers camped and drums beating.

A war almost did result from this; men were carrying arms to the site. There were fistfights. Finally, it was resolved by the state Supreme Court.

In a compromise, the militia was released from duty, and the Republicans met in the House while the Populists met elsewhere.

In 1894, Lewelling left the governor's office and came back to Wichita to continue his grocery and dairy business. In 1896, he entered the political arena again and was elected state senator from Sedgwick County.

He died in September 1900.

The Rajah Rabbitry

It was hare today, gone tomorrow

The Rajah Rabbitry at 3400 W. Douglas was billed as the greatest rabbitry in the world.

In the early summer of 1929, J.S. "Rajah" Porter arrived in town with 13 fluffy white rabbits. On July 1 of that year, he announced to The Wichita Beacon his plans for a hare farm, located in and around the vacated Kansas Sanitarium property, where he would breed a superior rabbit.

Shortly after that, he began confiding to Wichita residents that fortunes could be made. The local papers were full of one-page advertisements touting the benefits and moneymaking potential of the Rajah Rabbits.

"You can make for yourself an earning power of $40 to $60 a week, within a year, anywhere, raising Rajah Rabbits.

"We buy all the Rajah Rabbits you produce, at a guaranteed minimum price. You can start on as little as $80 and fifty square feet of space," the advertisements promised.

The Wichita Eagle on Feb. 9, 1930, devoted the front page to the Rajah Rabbit industry with a banner headline reading "Where Rabbit Is

Bob Rich remembers that June of 1930, when J.S. Porter left town.

King." The rest of the page was filled with stories noting the worth of the rabbits as well as a rabbit school Porter was opening where people could learn about caring for the animals.

News stories noted that the pelts of the animals were used in the manufacture of imitation chinchilla coats and the meat was sold for food. The papers also published recipes for fried rabbit, baked rabbit, rabbit stew and rabbit pie.

The man dealt with volume. The initial impact of the promotion was great and sharp. The citizens bought it.

Then, less than a year after Porter came to town, local residents discovered that he had loaded his maroon Packard with his personal belongings and left, leaving the rabbits to starve.

Bob Rich remembers all too well that June of 1930 when Porter mysteriously left town, leaving hundreds of rabbits starving.

"We read about them in the Friday afternoon newspaper. They had been abandoned," said Rich, who now lives in Riverside. "So, the next morning my folks and I went out—we stopped at the feed store and took jugs of water. I wanted to take them all home. I felt awful sorry for them."

Ellington said Porter's rabbitry

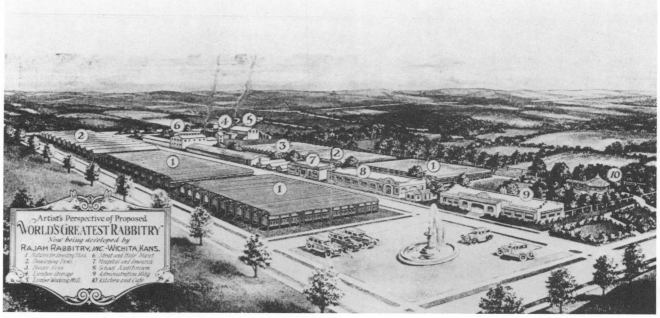

Less than a year after J.S. "Rajah" Porter arrived in Wichita, he abandoned his Rajah Rabbitry.

"was a flimflam operation that took advantage of the times and the people's investments. The fact that he so mysteriously disappeared, leaving his hares behind, starving and dying of lack of water, angered those who had invested. It dealt a blow to the community."

An article published in Harpers Journal on Jan. 27, 1973, recalled the rabbit operation: "Creditors flooded the Sedgwick County Court House with claims against its abandoned property, but its auction value of $13,000 was a mere token of the outstanding items which totaled almost one-half million dollars. Porter had sold animals and shares in his concern to more than 450 persons for a total of $340,000 and had left a sizable unsettled debt for assorted personal goods and rabbit food."

Wichita residents were stunned that the rabbitry wasn't being maintained.

No one knows for sure what happened to Rajah Porter, Ellington said, "Apparently he got away scot-free but we're not quite sure what he got away with."

The rabbitry was converted to a nightclub, The Green Tree Inn, in the '40s, and then razed several decades ago. Today, the property is part of the Mount Carmel apartment complex.

Soldiers, Scouts and Developers

"No section lines, or hedgerows, obstructed our path. Earth was as free as air, and water, and sunshine. The cattle on a thousand hills were ours."
—J.R. Mead, one of Wichita's developers

Indian scout signed an important peace treaty

Kit Carson didn't spend a lot of time in what is now Wichita during the 1860s, but what time he did spend in the city was important to the development of Kansas.

Carson—trapper, Indian scout and soldier—was one of the signers of the Little River Peace Treaty in 1865. He also was a mediator in the conference between the United States government and the Indian nations.

Although peace from the treaty was short-lived, the conference marked a step toward making the state safe for settlers. In addition, it allowed government officials to express concern over the Sand Creek Massacre, which took place the previous year. But one of the most significant aspects of the conference, according to local historians, was that it drew together some of the more powerful leaders of the Indian nations and the United States.

Carson's presence was an important factor. Both the government and the Indian leaders knew of him. He was a legend of the West. It was significant that he was a member of the commission in this treaty. This was the government's first main effort to have peace with the Indians.

Carson was born in Kentucky in 1809. His family moved to Missouri when he was less than a year old. He worked first as a saddler's apprentice, then after 1826 devoted himself to being a scout and hunter.

In 1828, he joined a party traveling to Santa Fe, N.M., which was his first trip across the Kansas territory. When the party stopped at Pawnee Rock near Great Bend, Carson, then 19, was frightened by the possibility of Indians. He is reported to

During his lifetime, Kit Carson became a well-known and respected figure on the frontier of the old American West.

have seen movement at night and, thinking it was Indians, accidentally shot his own mule.

Years later, by the time the Little River Peace Treaty was being formed, Carson had become an American legend and was considered by many to be of the same caliber as Daniel Boone.

The treaty conference took place on what is now the northwest corner of Seneca and 61st Street North. An account of the treaty, published in the Marion Record in 1913 by George Coble, indicates Carson arranged a prisoner exchange.

Coble was present during the treaty and said that chiefs from the Apache, Arapaho, Cheyenne, Comanche and Kiowa nations met with U.S. government officials.

A spokesman for the officials said

no agreement could be reached until the Indians returned their prisoners.

The Indians denied having any prisoners.

"Carson said to the Indians around the table, 'If the prisoners you have are not brought in, I am going to fight,' " Coble wrote.

Carson then appointed a plainsman, Charlie Rath, to take a group of Indians and bring back the prisoners. Rath's party brought in seven prisoners that had been captured in Black Jack, Texas.

Carson told Coble: "With Indians you are in the most danger when you feel the safest."

Each day of the negotiations, a messenger was sent from the site of the treaty to Fort Riley, near Junction City, to inform the government of progress.

The treaty forced the removal of the five Indian nations from Kansas into Indian Territory, now known as Oklahoma.

Carson died three years later of an aneurysm at Fort Lyon, Colo. The report of his doctor, H.R. Tilton, said Carson had grown weak from heart trouble and was bedridden the last few days of his life. During the middle of the afternoon on May 23, 1868, Carson asked for a buffalo steak and coffee. He ate, smoked his clay pipe, then suddenly called out, "Doctor! Compadre! Adios!"

He was dead.

Yet his role in shaping the West is still remembered.

"Carson's presence gave a feeling of security to those out in this area that maybe some accomplishments were going to take place," Ellington said. "He was respected on both sides of the fence."

J.R. Mead

He knew that history was being made as he lived

When pioneer settlement was just beginning at the confluence of the Arkansas and Little Arkansas rivers in 1868, James R. Mead suggested naming that gathering of houses and buildings "Wichita" after the Wichita Indians who had earlier occupied the area.

As one of the first pioneers and tradesmen in the area, Mead's word carried clout.

Mead knew many of the various traders in the country, as well as Indians. He was well-respected and well-known. He believed history was being made as he lived. He made sure his life was well-documented.

Mead was born in New Haven, Vt., in 1836. When he was 3, his family moved to Davenport, Iowa. He lived there until 1859, when at 23 he left home and traveled to Burlingame to begin trading with Indian tribes.

At that time, the territory of Kansas extended from the Missouri River to the crest of the Rocky Mountains. Mead explored the territory, became adept at hunting buffalo and soon established a trading

J.R. Mead became adept at hunting buffalo.

post at what is now Salina.

In 1863, he started trading posts near Towanda in Butler County and what is now 17th Street and the Little Arkansas River in Wichita.

In 1864 and 1868, he represented Butler County in the Kansas Legislature, and later represented a district comprising Morris, Chase, Marion and Butler counties plus the

unorganized territory west of the state line, which now covers about 35 counties.

Mead organized a company in 1871 to construct the Wichita & Southwestern Railroad, the first railroad in Wichita. About that same time, Mead and three other Wichita leaders—N.A. English, Mike Meagher and J.M. Steele—were instrumental in attracting Texas cattlemen to Wichita.

Mead was one of the key landowners of the original town. He had a quarter section of land that bordered Central to Douglas and Broadway to Washington. That was probably one of the key commercial properties in downtown Wichita. And because of that, he was instrumental in promoting Douglas Avenue.

His first house, a large brick structure, sat on the southeast corner of Central and Broadway.

Ellington said Mead was also one of the early presidents of the Kansas State Historical Society and devoted much of his time to preserving early Kansas history.

Mead's first wife, Agnes, died in 1869. He remarried in 1873, to Lucy Inman. She died in 1894. Two years later, he married Fern Hoover.

"He was a quiet man and was conservative," said the late Ignace Mead Jones, a daughter from that last marriage. "He wasn't one of the Wild West rough people. But he had a great love for Kansas and did everything he could to present the city and state. He was an adventurer."

As an early-day pioneer, Mead watched the prairie change. A Feb. 23, 1883, Wichita Weekly Beacon article quotes him as saying:

"No section lines, or hedgerows, obstructed our path. Earth was as free as air, and water, and sunshine. The cattle on a thousand hills were ours.

"These plains were covered with unnumbered myriads of buffalo. The wanton greed of the white man has slaughtered the last one. The

J.R. Mead's house sat on the southeast corner of Central and Broadway.

elk, the deer and the antelope have likewise disappeared. Our rivers and streams once swarmed with fish. Our water courses were skirted with noble groves of cotton-wood, walnut, hackberry, oak and elm. They are gone. Verily, to quote the remark of my Indian friend, Not-ta-tunka, the white man is a 'heap no good.' "

In the spring of 1910, Mead contracted a severe cold, which rapidly developed into pneumonia. On March 31 he died at his home.

William Mathewson

The original Buffalo Bill was larger than life

William Mathewson, the original Buffalo Bill, hated publicity.

A pioneer plainsman, Indian fighter and government scout, Mathewson was often approached by writers who offered to pay for his life story.

But Wichita's Buffalo Bill kept silent, only occasionally revealing anecdotes to a few close friends and family members. Those anecdotes, though, added up to a story that was larger than life.

By all the different accounts of

Later in his life, William Mathewson moved from his log house to this house at 1047 N. Market. He died there in 1916, at the age of 86.

William Mathewson, left, and William Cody, both known as Buffalo Bill, met in 1913 in Mathewson's pasture.

settlers in the 1860s, Mathewson's name became legend. That legend came forward again in the 1880s when the Denver papers were noting the fact that he was called Buffalo Bill.

Mathewson was born in New York state on Jan. 1, 1830. At 13 he was working in lumber camps and taking part in hunting expeditions into Michigan and Canada.

In 1853, he established a trading post near what is now Great Bend. He was there for 10 years and built other posts on the Santa Fe Trail between Independence, Mo., and Santa Fe, N.M.

The Indians called him "Sinpah Zillpah," meaning the "Long-Bearded, Dangerous Man." He earned the nickname after a fight with Kiowa chief Satanta.

During the drought of 1860, when crops failed and settlers were starving, Mathewson went hunting for buffalo and sent wagon trains of meat to the settlers.

Those who knew Mathewson called him Bill. The wagon teamsters picked up on the name and christened him Buffalo Bill.

In 1867, Mathewson was instrumental in arranging the Medicine Lodge Peace Treaty between the federal government and the Kiowa, Comanche, Apache, Arapaho and Cheyenne Indians.

Because of his knowledge of Indian sign language and of several Indian dialects, Mathewson is credited with returning more than 55 settlers, mostly women and children, from the Indians between 1854 and 1873.

Mathewson's frontier stories usually revolved around his favorite horse, a mare named Bess, who it was said could outrun anything in the country. One such story reported Mathewson riding Bess into an Indian battle to save a wagon train.

Mathewson came to Wichita in the spring of 1868 and claimed the area of land that is bordered by Washington, Hydraulic, Central and Douglas.

His log cabin, east of Wabash off Central, was one of the first houses to be built in Wichita.

He became recognized as a pillar of the community. In 1887, he organized and became president of the Wichita Savings Bank. He bought and sold cattle and had a controlling interest in the Motor Line of the Central Avenue and Eastern Street Railway. He also owned stock in the Fourth National Bank of Wichita, established a brick plant south of the city and opened an academy of music.

"Compared to his other lifestyle of trading and trailblazing on the Plains, I suppose to some degree he had a subdued life here," Ellington said. "But everyone still knew who he was, and he was still at the mainstream of life."

Although Mathewson never cared much for publicity, a contemporary of his, William Cody (also known as Buffalo Bill), did and became famous by touring the world at the turn of the century with Buffalo Bill's Wild West Show. It was reported in local papers that Wichita's Buffalo Bill despised the show. In 1913, the two met in Mathewson's pasture, near Central and Hydraulic.

Three years later, Mathewson died while sitting in a rocking chair in the home he had moved to at 1047 N. Market. He was 86.

The Grand Army of the Republic

Courthouse monument gave tribute to the "brethren"

In its day, the Grand Army of the Republic was a proud force in Wichita.

Composed of about 100 Union veterans of the Civil War, the group met periodically from 1870 to the late 1930s. The former soldiers marched in parades and attended funerals, as a reminder of their role in the War Between the States.

"This was a brotherhood," Ellington said. "It took in people of prominence and those not so prominent."

But as the "brethren" died, so did the Grand Army of the Republic. In 1949, the group held its last reunion.

The GAR's impact in Wichita can be seen at three sites: the south lawn of the Old Sedgwick County Courthouse, the Soldiers Circle at Maple Grove Cemetery and the Civil War section in Highland Cemetery.

Members were most proud of the courthouse monument. The group erected the $22,000 monument in 1913 and dedicated it to all Union soldiers.

Originally, the monument was to have been at the east end of the Douglas Avenue bridge, where the Ramada Hotel at Broadview Place now stands.

City business and government leaders reasoned that the monument would be seen there by all train passengers entering the city and by spectators at the newly constructed ballpark on Ackerman Island, north of the bridge.

But that site was not well-received. It was abandoned when supporters decided the monument would need a 16-foot foundation in the sand along the banks of the Arkansas River.

Also, the site was criticized by Wichita artist John Noble, a nationally famous painter. He said it would be more appropriate for another statue and suggested a Wichita Indian chief commanding the view of the two rivers. His suggestion finally bore fruit when the Keeper of the Plains was completed 62 years later by another Wichita artist, Blackbear Bosin.

After the Douglas site was abandoned, the GAR supporters considered Central Riverside Park but eventually chose the lawn of the old courthouse.

The monument is 50 feet high and has an inner chamber to house artifacts and displays. Each of the four statues on the lower pedestal is 6½ feet high.

The memorial was designed by E.M. Viquesny, an artist in Americus, Ga. The Woodbury Granite Co. of Hardwick, Vt., was contracted to supply the granite and marble.

Crowning the memorial is a 14-foot Goddess of Liberty.

In January 1913, the goddess was

The Goddess of Liberty, on the south lawn of the old courthouse, was turned to face Central.

Anthony Reed/The Wichita Eagle

the brunt of several media jokes. She originally faced the courthouse.

Several citizens wanted the statue turned to face Central Avenue. The headlines on The Wichita Beacon on Jan. 25, 1913, read, "Goddess Turns Her Back on Us, She Gazes Squarely at the Court House, Public Must Be Satisfied With a Rear View."

Finally submitting to pressure, local officials had the statue turned to face the south, costing the county an additional $100 to reset the bolts.

On June 14, 1913, the statue was unveiled. And, in 1988, when the courthouse celebrated its 100th anniversary, lights were installed to illuminate the memorial at night.

"It is one of the very finest of Civil War memorials in the United States," Ellington said.

Col. E.E. and Erwin Bleckley

Father-and-son team earned city's respect

Shortly after the turn of the century, Wichita residents held the Bleckley men in high regard—Col. E.E., the father, and Erwin, his son.

Wichitans admired the father because he was a prominent business leader in the community. And they loved the son because he was a World War I hero.

Col. Bleckley had a lot to do with improving railroad services to Wichita. "The son was definitely a hero because he gave his life during the war; he helped place Wichita on the map," Ellington said. "People were very proud of him."

The elder Bleckley came to Wichita during the 1880s. For more than 20 years, he was the city passenger agent for the Missouri Pacific Railroad.

He married Margaret Alice Littell in 1892. She was a founder and active member of St. James Episcopal Church. She also served on the first board of directors of the YWCA. Erwin was the couple's only child.

After his work with the Missouri Pacific, Bleckley started working with Fourth National Bank. At the time of his death, in November 1931, he was the bank's vice president.

The Wichita Eagle reported on Nov. 30, 1931, that Bleckley "had the ability of making friends and holding them. Those who knew him . . . spoke of his congenial spirit and his sense of humor which made him a sparkling conversationalist. He was widely read and highly educated."

Likewise, people spoke highly of his son.

Business leader E.E. Bleckley was drawn by A.G. Allen for The Wichita Eagle of Jan. 14, 1910.

Erwin Bleckley was one of only four American fliers to be awarded the Medal of Honor during World War I.

Lt. Erwin Bleckley was one of only four American fliers to be awarded the Medal of Honor during World War I.

Erwin Bleckley was raised in Wichita and was one of the first men in the area to volunteer for World War I.

During one of the more famous battles of the war, the U.S. 77th division, which became known as the Lost Battalion, was surrounded by Germans in the Argonne Forest in France.

Bleckley and Lt. Harold Goettler, members of the 50th Observation Squadron, repeatedly flew their plane over the battle site to drop supplies to the Americans.

The Eagle reported that as Bleckley leaned over to survey the ground, every German rifle and machine gun within range turned loose on him.

"For a moment the enemy forgot all else," the paper reported. "This lone plane over them signified what they hated and wanted to overcome, and at it they hurled thousands of bullets with all the skill they had.

"Goettler skidded his plane, he made startling turns, he side-slipped a little occasionally, he climbed and he dived. Each time the plane turned and its great mottled belly flopped back into normal position, the men of the Lost Battalion groaned and expected to see it tumble from the sky.

"But on its way it went like a charmed thing, roaring up and down and across, rocked occasionally by the ash of big shells that had just passed."

Bleckley poured a burst of lead into a German machine-gun nest. And all day the men of the Lost Battalion watched and waited.

The men "had lain there in their holes, watching bundle after bundle of food and supplies drop just below them, barely out of reach."

The plane finally was hit and crashed into the French terrain.

Bleckley exemplified bravery for Wichita residents at that time. His name is not forgotten today. It is brought up often on Memorial Day as one of the local heroes.

Today what remains of the family's name is Bleckley Drive, a street in southeast Wichita, named in honor of Erwin.

Woodrow Wilson

The president made the trip but not the speech

In 1919, when Wichitans heard that the president of the United States was coming to town, they worked hard to give him a welcome.

Committees were formed and it was decided that President Woodrow Wilson would give his speech at the Forum, the forerunner of Century II, at English and Water.

On Sept. 26, 1919, 100,000 Kansans gathered to hear Wilson speak. It was the largest crowd ever assembled in the city. But Wilson was seriously ill the morning his train pulled into Wichita. He never left the presidential car. And no one from Wichita saw him.

That's why The Wichita Eagle called it "The Wilsonless Day."

It was a disappointment. "People came from all areas around to see the president," Ellington said. "Schoolchildren were even waving little flags. It was a day of mixed emotions."

At the beginning of September 1919, Wilson was pushing hard to get the United States into the League of Nations. To gain support, he did an extensive tour of the western United States by train in his presidential car, the blue "Mayflower." He toured and spoke in almost every state west of the Mississippi.

The president's special party included Mrs. Wilson, the president's personal physician, a maid, eight Secret Service men, two dozen reporters and a double train crew.

Almost as soon as the tour was

President Woodrow Wilson never regained his health.

announced, residents in Wichita began preparing for Wilson's visit. The stop was to be the next to the last in the tour. From Wichita, Wilson was expected to go on to Oklahoma City.

Schools were dismissed and children, dressed in costumes of the Allied Nations and Uncle Sam, lined Douglas Avenue. The president was scheduled to tour College Hill, see a wheat show and attend a parade.

But the trip was exhaustive, and the president began to show signs of ill health early on. Headlines from The Wichita Beacon reported the president "had a headache past nine days."

"President Wilson is not one to complain of feeling ill and it is very

Cars lined up in front of Union Depot Station to take President Woodrow Wilson to the Forum, the forerunner of Century II.

unusual for him to have a headache. All through his address yesterday at Pueblo, Colo., Mrs. Wilson closely watched the face of her husband for fear that he might show some signs of weakness and be compelled to give up his address."

It was 9 a.m. Sept. 26, 1919, when the presidential train arrived in Wichita. It pulled onto a siding just south of 10th and Santa Fe and stopped.

It didn't proceed to Union Station as planned, because during the night, between Pueblo and Wichita, Wilson had become gravely ill.

He had suffered a partial stroke and nervous exhaustion.

From a small grocery store at 714 E. 10th, Wilson's physician, Cary Grayson, called Western Union and dictated several telegrams to Washington on the president's health.

At 9:45 a.m., the waiting crowd was told Wilson was unable to make his speech because of illness.

The people slowly drifted away.

The president's train left Wichita at 11:27 a.m. for Newton to proceed east. It arrived in Washington two days later. Wilson never regained his health and served the remainder of his term as an invalid. He died Feb. 3, 1924. His proposal to include the United States in the League of Nations died as well.

A.A. Hyde

Philanthropist left an aroma of Mentholatum

In 1925, when Albert Alexander Hyde of Wichita celebrated his 77th birthday, 1,150 people from 14 states attended a dinner in his honor, and another 3,000 came to applaud the success of the city's favorite philanthropist.

Many of the people were local civic leaders, but many people came from the various YMCAs throughout the country that Hyde helped start through his contributions. Others came from cities where his plants were situated. And still others were political leaders, such as the governor of Colorado.

"He was a very well-loved man, locally and elsewhere," Ellington said. "He had a charitable attitude and he would talk to anyone at any level. He was a pioneer of employers in that he was one of the first who provided a facility for his workers to relax during their lunch period."

Albert Alexander Hyde chose to share his wealth.

Hyde first gained international attention as the manufacturer of Mentholatum, a mixture of menthol and petrolatum. His product, which originated in Wichita, still is sold today. The company headquarters is in Buffalo, N.Y.

Hyde later was known for his charitable works for more than 60 organizations. He helped found Wichita's YMCA and YWCA, and helped build the YMCA camp in Estes Park, Colo. Other works he contributed to included the Henry Roe Cloud Indian Institute, the Wichita Children's Home, Wesley Hospital and Nurses Training School.

Hyde believed in giving away nine-tenths of his salary. His money went to charitable organizations because he wanted to share his wealth.

Born in 1848 in Lee, Mass., Hyde came to Kansas in 1865 and worked as a bookkeeper for a Leavenworth bank. In July 1872, the bank sent Hyde to Wichita to open the Wichita Savings Bank. He then moved to the Farmers and Merchants Bank, which later became the First National Bank of Wichita.

By 1887, he had established himself as a private banker. The owner of various real estate holdings, he was considered one of the wealthier men in the city. But his wealth from real estate soon dissolved when Wichita's economy hit bottom, leaving him bankrupt.

Then, in 1889, Hyde began a toilet soap business, the Yucca Co., along with his brother-in-law, Clayton K. Smith, a pharmacist, and Walter R. Binkley.

In May 1890, Hyde bought out his partners and began experimenting with a menthol-based salve, which he prepared on the family stove. The Mentholatum business was prospering by the turn of the century, and Hyde dissolved the Yucca Co. in November 1906 and created the Mentholatum Co.

The Mentholatum building still stands at the northeast corner of Cleveland and Douglas.

Hyde died in 1935 at age 87.

The old Mentholatum building at Douglas and Cleveland, built in 1908, was the first steel-reinforced concrete building in Wichita.

Governors,
Lawyers
and Cooks

"I want to die in the harness. I've been fighting all my life, and I couldn't bear the inactivity of a long illness. I'm not afraid of death, but I want it to come quickly, when it does come."
—Col. Sam Amidon

Patrick Valentine Healy

For him the church bells tolled

Patrick Valentine Healy was a staunch Irish Catholic who loved the sound of a church bell on Sunday mornings.

He came to Wichita in 1876 because the residents rang their bells proudly.

Healy, who dealt in real estate, originally settled on a farm near Wellington. But, he said in an article from the May 14, 1911, Wichita Eagle, the town had no church bells.

"Folks going to church without the ringing of a bell didn't make Sunday seem right," he told a newspaper reporter when asked why he settled in Wichita. "I made up my mind that I would not stay in Wellington very many more Sundays without a bell, so I wrote out a subscription paper and started it off with $5."

The townspeople of Wellington didn't care if they had a bell or not, and Healy became outraged.

"I tore up the petition right there and said that I wouldn't stay in a town that didn't have any more public-spirited citizens than Wellington has had," Healy said. "Soon afterwards I rode into Wichita on a freight wagon, traded my farm for a house and lot, and I have never regretted the move."

During the 1870s and the 1880s, Healy was one of Wichita's leading real estate dealers. He and two partners, H.O. Meigs and Nicholas F. Neiderlander, conducted an insurance business on the side of the real estate boom. Healy was also a

Patrick Valentine Healy was a leading real estate dealer.

farmer-stockman. His office was at 422 E. Douglas.

In 1886, the book "Wichita, Its Progress and Importance" reported on Healy: "A large portion of the real estate transactions are through the hands of Mr. Healy and his list shows decided bargains at all times. In addition, he is fully prepared to pay taxes, collect rents, negotiate loans and place insurance."

Ellington described Healy as a reliable businessman:

"When he hooked up with Neiderlander, who was the biggest real estate dealer of all, Healy was at the zenith of his career. He was a

well-respected man who attracted anyone who was interested in real estate. People loved him to show the lots. I would guess he was a very outgoing, friendly man."

Old newspaper accounts indicate that Healy was born on Feb. 14, 1848, in Scott, Ky., and that he lived in Kentucky until 1855, when his family moved to Illinois. His descendants, however, say he was born in Ireland and later came to the United States.

The 1888 "Biographical Album of Wichita and Sedgwick County" said Healy not only was involved in Wichita's real estate but also made bricks. Twenty-five men worked for him.

He was a large stockholder and director of the State National Bank, and a stockholder in the Wichita Watch Factory, the Kansas Sash and Door Co. and the Wichita Soap Manufactory.

Besides being a mover and shaker in the community, Healy was also a man who set records. The Wichita Eagle reported in an article that during an 1886 hailstorm, Healy saw a huge hailstone.

It measured 13½ inches in circumference, or more than 4¼ inches in diameter. He took the hailstone to his office and put it on the scales. It weighed a pound and a half—a hefty stone in anyone's books.

Healy died in 1918. He is buried in the Calvary Catholic Cemetery near Kellogg and Hillside.

Nathaniel English

City developer was a kingpin of the community

From the beginning, Nathaniel English was a mover and shaker.

He bought land, dabbled in politics, and built businesses, railroads and banks. The end result: He went

down in Wichita's history books as one of the city's primary developers.

English came to Kansas in 1861 from Ohio, locating in Leavenworth, where he began trad-

ing with the Kiowas and Arapahos. Kiowa Chief Satanta once kidnapped English, then later released him when English's friends paid the ransom.

In 1870, English arrived in Wich-

Nathaniel English was on the first Sedgwick County Commission.

ita. He opened the city's first land office. Before long, he acquired the quarter section bounded by what is now Douglas, Kellogg, Broadway and Washington. English was the one who suggested Wichita's business street be named after his friend, Illinois politician Stephan A. Douglas, who ran against Abraham Lincoln in the presidential election of 1860.

From 1874 to 1878, English helped build one of the largest elevators of that time in the Arkansas Valley. And it was his company that shipped the first train carload of wheat from the city.

English was later president and owned stock in the city's Street Railway Co. He also owned stock in the Brunswick Stone Works, the stockyards and a hotel. He was involved in local banking and owned real estate in Butler, Chase, McPherson, Sumner and Kingman counties.

By reputation he became one of the kingpins of the community. Like J.R. Mead and William Greiffenstein, English helped build the community.

When disputes between white settlers and Indians arose, English served as a mediator. In the spring of 1870, when an Arapaho warrior carried off a child, town fathers gathered to plan her rescue.

An alarm was sounded and a crowd of businessmen and cowboys gathered in front of the Occidental Hotel at Second and Main. William Mathewson, the original Buffalo Bill; English and the girl's father trailed the Arapahos to camp, where they offered a knife and a silver half-dollar in exchange for Rea Woodman.

Their mission was to receive the girl and not stir up any problems with the Indians.

They were successful.

Woodman later wrote about the experience in her book, "Wichitana."

English served on the first Sedgwick County Commission, beginning in April 1870. The commission's first action was to serve notice that within 30 days, all cattle would have to be confined at night.

Cattle continued to be an issue into the spring of 1870, when a power struggle sprang up between Park City and Wichita officials. Both cities wanted the business from Texas cattlemen, and both cities wanted to be recognized as the county seat.

At that time, Park City was directly west of Valley Center off the Arkansas River.

English was one of four horsemen to ride out and meet Texas cattlemen on the trail and persuade them to bring their herds and business through Wichita.

"Park City officials were throwing out erroneous information that Chisholm Creek was poisonous to cattle and would make them ill," Ellington said. "By persuasion, the four Wichita horsemen offered to pay double the amount for any cattle lost along the Wichita route."

The cattle came to Wichita, and the city was soon known as a cow town.

But when the bust of 1889 hit the city, English suffered severely. He never fully recovered from the financial blow.

English lived on the northwest corner of Lewis and Topeka and died Aug. 4, 1892.

Nathaniel English lived on the northwest corner of Lewis and Topeka. He was in a group that urged Texas cattlemen to bring their business to Wichita.

Robert Lawrence

His Palace Block building was an "architect's dream"

For years, the building known as the Palace Block was one of the city's showpieces—thanks to Robert Lawrence.

Described as an "architect's dream," the building at Seneca and Douglas was constructed of brick, stone and granite, and its top stories sported 18 stained-glass bay windows.

The Palace Block was built in the mid-1880s by Lawrence, an early Wichita capitalist and landowner, and was designed by the city's premier architects of the time—Willis Proudfoot and George Washington Bird.

During their six-year residence in Wichita, the two designed 29 city projects: two banks, 13 commercial structures, three university projects, three schools, six residences, one factory and one YMCA. Only nine remain.

Still standing in North Newton is another of their projects, the administration building at Bethel College.

Their buildings in Wichita were typically massive structures, featuring arches, turrets, curved porches and stone-faced masonry.

The Palace Block, a business and office building, was no exception. It featured a skylight and open courtyard inside the building. It was built at the then-heady cost of $29,000.

"I think the name gave it prestige," Ellington said. "It implies what it appeared to be—a palace on the west side. I went in and saw it when they were tearing it down in 1972. The workers who were dismantling the upper portion of the building made the remark that they felt squeamish destroying something like that, because of the very fine work that had gone into it."

The idea for the Palace came from Lawrence.

He was instrumental in bringing the Frisco and Missouri Pacific railroads to Wichita. He platted his farm on the west side and developed seven additions to the city.

Lawrence had large banking interests in Kansas. He was at one time a director of the Kansas National Bank, and also a director of the National Bank of Pratt.

He came to Wichita in 1870 from Connecticut. He traveled by foot through Connecticut, Massachu-

Lawrence Elementary and Lawrence-Dumont Stadium are named for Robert Lawrence.

setts and New York, selling stenciled drawings until he had made enough money for transportation to Illinois. Once there, he bought a team of horses that he then drove to Wichita.

Newspaper clippings say Lawrence's first house was made of logs and had an earthen roof. But investments in real estate soon made him a wealthy man. So wealthy that in the 1880s, he replaced his simple home with a $70,000 stone mansion at the corner of Seneca and Maple. He sold that house to the Masonic Lodge in 1896. Twenty years later, the house was destroyed by fire.

Lawrence was elected to the state Legislature in 1884. He served two terms and was also a member of the school board.

Born on Dec. 17, 1847, in Litchfield, Conn., he died on Jan. 28, 1921, at his home at 1011 N. Topeka, which no longer stands. Lawrence Elementary School and Lawrence-Dumont Stadium are both named for him.

The Palace Block had 18 stained-glass bay windows, a skylight and an open courtyard. It was built in the mid-1880s for the then-heady cost of $29,000.

Thomas Fitch

Businessman had his hand in 25 corporations

Thomas Fitch was only 25 when he came to Wichita to start work as an investment broker.

Before he was through, he became involved with more than 25 corporations. His accomplishments read like a resume:

Fitch was manager of the Riverside & Suburban Railway from 1887 to 1890; general manager of the Wichita Electric Railway Co. from 1890 to 1893; general manager of the Larned Water Works from 1887 to 1893; and general manager of the El Dorado Water Works from 1892 to 1904.

He also was one of the city's first postmasters, appointed by President Grover Cleveland in 1894. He served until May 1898.

"He was not what I would call a mover and shaker but a blender," Ellington said. "He was a good communicator and one who was easy to work with, but personality-wise he was not as colorful as other leaders during that time. Yet, he was one of the men who pushed Wichita's economy along during the 1880s."

Fitch was born in Bristol, Maine, on April 9, 1861. His father, Maj. Joseph Fitch, fought in the Civil War with the 20th Maine Volunteer Infantry. At the close of the war, he moved his family to Chicago. The Fitches were in Illinois only a few years when, in 1871, they moved to El Dorado.

That Kansas connection is probably what caused Fitch to move to Wichita in 1886.

"He was well aware of the boom here; that truly was what attracted him here," Ellington said.

Fitch's home at 901 Spaulding was the first in Wichita to be wired for electric lights.

The house, which still stands, is known as Riverside Cottage. It is listed as a local and state landmark, and it is on the National Register of Historic Places.

It was constructed in 1887 by architects Willis Proudfoot and George Washington Bird. A carved panel in the stone chimney on the north side of the front gable contains the dwelling's name and a gargoyle's face appears between the lettering.

"(Fitch) was a good communicator and one who was easy to work with."

Thomas Fitch's home at 901 Spaulding was the first in Wichita to be wired for electric lights; it still stands and is known as Riverside Cottage.

Dave Williams/The Wichita Eagle

Early on, Fitch established a business friendship with his brother-in-law, J.O. Davidson. Together the two started the Riverside & Suburban Railway, one of the nation's first electric street railway systems.

Fitch was instrumental in promoting housing developments in Riverside. He was also owner of the Western Pacific Tea Co.

Aside from his business negotiations, Fitch had one major main interest. He was a Mason. He was grandmaster of the Masons in Kansas and grandmaster of the local chapter, council and commandery.

During the Spanish-American War, Fitch became a colonel, leading the 21st Kansas volunteer infantry in 1898.

Fitch died on March 12, 1938. He is buried in Old Mission Mausoleum.

Benajah Aldrich

As mayor, he led city through its boom

Benajah Aldrich and his home made a mark in Wichita's history.

As mayor from 1885 to 1887, during the city's boom period, Aldrich brought two railroads to Wichita and annexed the town of Delano—the area west of the Arkansas River that had served as a "pop-off valve" for cowboys during the 1870s.

Alrich was known for his ability to manage affairs of the city. He had an open-door philosophy and was easily reached by his patrons.

Aldrich was born in Kalamazoo, Mich., in 1846. He came to Wichita in 1870 and began a career as a pharmacist. His drugstore, Aldrich & Brown, was at 142 N. Main. During his first decade in Wichita, Aldrich was also the deputy postmaster of Wichita and served on the City Council from 1876 to 1878.

"As Mr. Aldrich was one of Wichita's foremost citizens, he was more or less thrown into politics," the Wichita Daily Beacon reported on Feb. 18, 1907. "He was known as a broad thinker on governmental questions. . . . He performed the duties of mayor accurately and faithfully. His office was made a few months later very arduous as it was this year the boom, in all its fury, struck Wichita."

The city's population in 1885 increased by about 20,000 people. Millions of dollars were spent on public and private improvements. One of the nation's first electric railroads, the Riverside Line, was built by J.O. Davidson. Linwood Park was laid out, and a city fire marshal's office was created.

Ellington said Aldrich also had the ability to accomplish big things personally. His home became one of Wichita's finest during the 1880s.

"He was a good manager of his financial affairs, which was demonstrated by his home," Ellington

Benajah and Anna Aldrich built a three-story brick and limestone house at 3800 E. Douglas, the site now occupied by Blessed Sacrament Church.

Benajah Aldrich "was universally respected for his integrity."

said. "It was the showcase of College Hill and was built to stimulate finer homes in that section."

Aldrich and his wife, Anna, built the three-story brick and limestone house at 3800 E. Douglas, the site now occupied by Blessed Sacrament Church. The Catholic Church bought the house from the Aldriches in 1900. Bishop John Hennessy lived in the house until 1920.

Aldrich died Feb. 17, 1907, from blood poisoning.

"Mr. Aldrich was a member of the Chamber of Commerce and took an active interest in all affairs of importance to the city," The Wichita Eagle reported on Feb. 19, 1907. "He was universally respected for his integrity in all matters, both public and private, and the news of his death came as a shock to the many who knew him. The flag at the city building was hung at half-mast in his honor."

James Oakley Davidson

Banker served as a city booster during the boom

In 1886, when Wichita was at the height of its boom period, The Wichita Eagle ran a list of the 43 wealthiest men in town.

James Oakley Davidson, with $400,000 worth of assets, ranked second to C.R. Miller's $500,000. Davidson was a successful local banker and investor who capitalized on Wichita's growth during the 1880s.

Davidson was the inspiration for the Riverside district by developing the Riverside Land Company. He was also one of Wichita's early town boosters. He made a habit of promoting Wichita and going East to get different capitalists involved in enterprises.

Davidson arrived in Wichita by stagecoach in 1872. In 1883, he bought the northwest corner of Main and Douglas and organized the Citizens State Bank, of which he was elected president. He also opened a racing track west of the Arkansas River, in what is now the Central Riverside Park area. He then built a bridge to Riverside, now the Murdock Street bridge.

In January 1887, Davidson was credited with encouraging a New York company to build 2½ miles of electric streetcar lines in Wichita, one of the first such systems in the United States.

And later that year, when the Burton Stock Car Co. was looking for a place to build its shops, Davidson persuaded the company to locate near Wichita by giving it 70 acres of land and agreeing to be responsible for a bonus of $200,000.

The Burton Stock Car Co., at

James Oakley Davidson was the second wealthiest man in Wichita a century ago.

what is now 801 E. 37th N., manufactured livestock railroad cars and at one time employed 550 people. Today, the Coleman Co. maintains a plant in the complex.

"It was almost a city in itself simply because of its magnitude," Ellington said.

But the stock car company never lived up to the hopes of the townspeople. The local economy plummeted in 1889. And though the company continued for a few more years, it abandoned the five-building complex after 1893.

"It wasn't nearly as significant as it was expected to be," said Edward Tihen, now deceased. He was a retired Wichita physician who researched the company. "It never did have the volume or the employees that were expected. But it was, for a time, something that local pro-

The Burton Stock Car Co. employed 550, but in six years never fulfilled its potential. It manufactured livestock railroad cars.

moters could point to when they were trying to draw other businesses here."

Ellington said the Burton Stock Car Co. "was our first taste of heavy industry into our area. It placed the bread on many tables during that period of time."

And it was through Davidson, Ellington said, that local industry was nurtured and boosted. "He gave our early industry a shot in the arm."

Ola Martinson

Real estate was his forte

In Wichita's early days, Ola Martinson was blessed with the right combination:

He knew where to buy land and when to sell it.

Martinson was a good land speculator. He took advantage of the boom that was going on, and was well-liked by the community.

Martinson was born Sept. 20, 1844, on a farm in southern Sweden. In 1866, he traveled to Chicago, where he worked as a laborer. He came to Wichita in July 1870 and for a few months helped operate a flour and feed business. He then worked at a bakery for several years.

One of the opportunities Martinson took advantage of was the Homesteader's Act, which allowed individuals to obtain 160 acres of land if they promised to develop it.

He sold his share of the bakery and moved to a claim seven miles west of Wichita on the Cowskin Creek. There he planted fruit and ornamental trees, built a house and married.

In 1883, Martinson purchased 240 acres in west Wichita for $12,000.

The Wichita Eagle reported on Oct. 3, 1920, that he "had the nerve, foresight and acumen to invest in 240 acres of land on the West Side, exactly where the Missouri Pacific had to cross in 1885 and 1886 to reach Hutchinson and Anthony."

When Martinson sold the 240 acres, he used the profits to start in the real estate business.

He acquired parcels of land and began buying and selling adjoining property. He built the Martinson Block, on the northwest corner of Seneca and Douglas. That block, in later years, became the Wichita Hospital. Martinson also built the West Side Hotel, 1200 W. Douglas, near where the Bayouth Super Market stands today.

Martinson owned stores and tenement houses in west Wichita, as well as the streetcar stables in the 400 block of North Seneca.

"His rise occurred because he was a wise investor," Ellington said. "He seemed to have the vision to know a good investment and how it would turn for him."

Martinson then built one of the more prestigious homes in Wichita, at 313 N. Seneca. The home was later purchased by Ben McLean, an early-day Wichita mayor. The Wichita Hospital owned the house after McLean and converted it into a nurses' home. The house was razed in 1960.

Martinson died in 1927 from

Martinson "seemed to have the vision to know a good investment and how it would turn for him."

heart failure. He is buried in Highland Cemetery.

A street in west Wichita was named in his honor.

Ola Martinson built one of the more prestigious houses in Wichita, at 313 N. Seneca.

Henry Allen

Even in France, he chalked up the votes

At times, Henry Allen couldn't believe his popularity.

"If six men get together and all six are for me, I'll call it an uprising," he told his supporters.

Well, more than six men were for him in the election for Kansas governor in 1918. Allen won by a landslide and became one of the state's most popular governors. He carried all but two of the state's 105 counties in his race against Albert Lansdon, a Democrat.

Born in Corry, Pa., in September 1869, Allen soon moved with his family to a farm in northeastern Kansas. He attended public schools in Clay and Osage counties and eventually became a barber. From his earnings, he saved enough to attend Baker University.

While at Baker, he became interested in journalism and, in 1891, started managing the Salina Republican. Three years later, when the paper was sold, he bought the Manhattan Nationalist. He sold it in 1896 and bought the Ottawa Herald and the Salina Republican. Allen changed the name of the Republican to the Salina Journal. Ten years later, he sold both papers and became editor and publisher of The Wichita Beacon. On July 4, 1928, he sold The Beacon to Max Levand.

Allen's position in journalism almost always kept him in the public's eye. And in 1917, when state

Henry Allen "was progressive in politics but he wasn't easily persuaded on any venture."

political leaders gathered to decide the Republican candidate for governor, Allen was a logical choice.

But war was brewing in Europe, and Allen left for France as organizer and superintendent of the Home Communication Service of the American Red Cross.

He was still in France when the election rolled around.

His absence for both the nomination and the election is the only such instance in the state's history. At the Continental Hotel in Paris on Nov. 10, 1918, Allen was handed a Paris edition of an American newspaper that told of his landslide election on Nov. 5.

The fact that Allen won the election while in France "shows the man was dedicated to his country," Ellington said. "The country was first, in front of his personal gain."

Allen served as Kansas governor from 1919 to 1923. He was appointed to the U.S. Senate in 1929 to take the place of Charles Curtis, who resigned to run for vice president.

Later, when he retired from politics, Allen and his wife, Elsie, became collectors of art. Their interest in art prompted them to become charter members of the Wichita Art Association. Their home at Second and Roosevelt also attracted much attention; Frank Lloyd Wright was hired to design it.

The Japanese-style, buff-brick house, completed in 1919, was the last of 200 that Wright designed in his trademark Prairie style. It is expected to open as a museum.

"Allen stands out over many of our governors through the years," Ellington said. "He was known for his steadfastness. He was progressive in politics but he wasn't easily persuaded on any venture. . . . That's what made him popular with the people. He had a charisma about him."

Allen died Jan. 17, 1950.

A.W. and Charles Bitting

Brothers kept Wichitans dressed in style

A.W. and Charles Bitting came to Wichita from the East Coast in 1877, determined to make a living on the Western frontier.

The brothers opened a modest clothing store, Keystone Clothing House, on the northwest corner of Douglas and Market. Within two years, it proved so successful that they expanded and renamed the business the Bitting Brothers One-Price Clothiers, Hatters & Furnishers.

In June 1884, The Wichita Eagle reported that the Bitting brothers were shrewd businessmen and excellent buyers.

"On counters arranged down through the center and main part of the room is a mammoth display of clothing of all styles, sizes and quality, except the shoddy, which is excluded," the paper said.

Charles, left, and Alfred Bitting—who went by A.W.—came from the East Coast determined to make a success of themselves.

Zero-degree weather soon put an ice shield on the four-story Bitting Building, which caught fire in January 1911.

On May 11, 1888, the brothers made the news again when The Daily Beacon reported that the "Bitting brothers have distributed the new police uniforms, and they have proven more than satisfactory to the force. The new uniforms will do much to smarten up the appearance of the men."

That reputation of quality continued to grow, and in 1887 the brothers temporarily relocated their store so they could build a four-story, brick and iron building on the Douglas and Market site. Upon completion, it was considered by local leaders to be one of the most impressive architectural structures in town.

"It was the ultimate as far as clothing houses in Wichita at that time," Ellington said. "It was looked upon with a great deal of awe by the people."

That next year, the brothers printed a brochure that featured pictures and stories about their building. It included photos of elaborate ornamental glass cases for merchandise.

But on Jan. 11, 1911, the building caught fire and burned. It was zero-degree weather, and even though firefighters tried desperately to extinguish the blaze, the outer walls were soon encased in ice.

Almost immediately after the fire, the brothers had plans drawn and work ordered to rebuild the first four floors of the building. In 1919, seven additional floors were added to bring the building to its present 11-story height.

The bricks used in the 1919 addition are slightly darker in color than those used on the lower floors. The addition line is visible about two feet above the fourth-floor windows.

The Bitting Building was extensively renovated and modernized in 1959. It continues to house offices and small shops.

Charles Bitting died in October 1932. A.W. died July 10, 1934.

Orsemus Hills Bentley

He laid the tracks for railway development

Orsemus Hills Bentley was an imposing man who raised pigs, practiced law and politics, spoke Spanish and recorded local history. And not long after he arrived in Wichita in 1880, Bentley became an imposing figure in the city's activities.

Although Bentley was one of the leading attorneys in Wichita and one of the big promoters of the city during the boom period, he was best known for his work on the history of Wichita and Sedgwick County.

Originally from New York state, Bentley taught school and practiced law in Columbus, Ohio, before coming to Kansas. Once in Wichita, he was the promoter and principal builder of the Kansas Midland Railway from Wichita to Ellsworth, and he assisted in promoting other railway enterprises. He also was an attorney for the Missouri Pacific railway.

Bentley served in the state Legislature from 1887 to 1891 and was mayor of Wichita from 1915 to 1916.

One of his early passions was documenting the "History of Wichita and Sedgwick County Kansas" in a two-volume account of early pioneers and their activities.

He also was known to enjoy free time. Old newspaper accounts report Bentley would close his law practice on hot summer afternoons and go swimming in the Little Arkansas River. He was a farmer who specialized in Hereford cattle and Poland-China hogs. At other times, he made news by commenting on items of the day.

"He always had an item of news, always had the faculty of judging accurately of its comparative importance and more often than not sat down and wrote it out for the mere love of doing it," The Wichita Eagle reported on Jan. 23, 1927.

The town of Bentley in the northwest portion of Sedgwick County was named in honor of Bentley because of his contributions to the railroad. In 1887, the Kansas Midland Railway was built from Wichita to Ellsworth. The railroad intersected the township, and a depot was constructed with Bentley's name.

Bentley and his wife, Flora, lived in Riverside, at 927 Litchfield. He

Orsemus Hills Bentley wrote a history of Wichita.

died on Jan. 22, 1927, from pneumonia. She died in 1940.

"Wichita has never known a man possessed of a greater diversity of talent than Orsemus Hills Bentley," The Eagle reported at the time of his death. "He was a strikingly effective advocate: an able man on the platform, a facile one with his pen."

William Stanley

As 15th governor, he promoted the state

William Stanley's career was marked by hard work, perseverance and a touch of star quality.

It took the latter for him to become the 15th governor of Kansas.

Stanley was the second Wichitan to be elected to the state office, serving from 1899 to 1902. Lorenzo Lewelling, the first, was Kansas' 12th governor, from 1893 to 1894.

Stanley was a local favorite.

"He excelled as one of our more prominent attorneys in Wichita. He had a following of friends and associates," Ellington said. "And a lot of those had a great hand in electing him governor. Along with that fact, he was a man who never seemed to create any negativism. He didn't have a lot of enemies, if any."

Stanley was born Dec. 28, 1844, in Knox County, Ohio. His father, a physician, encouraged him to get an education. So Stanley became a lawyer. In 1872 he came to Wichita. He was county attorney of Sedgwick County for three terms, then was elected to the state Legislature. He served one term in the state House.

Stanley then moved back to Wichita and maintained a successful career as an attorney. He supported development in the Riverside area, which at that time was outside Wichita's city limits. He and his wife, Emma, built a home on the southwest corner of Gilman and Riverside Avenue. It was razed in 1929 and replaced by a brick house that is a private residence.

In June 1898, at the Republican state convention in Hutchinson, Stanley was nominated for governor.

William Stanley was Sedgwick County attorney for three terms.

William Stanley and his wife, Emma, built their home at the southwest corner of Gilman and Riverside Avenue. In 1929, it was razed and replaced by a brick house that still stands.

He was elected by a large majority.

Stanley's years as governor were marked by railroad expansion and economic recovery. He also capitalized on the state's natural resources, promoting the state whenever he could.

"He was concerned about the success of the state," Ellington said. "He approached his role as governor much like one would with a Chamber of Commerce."

After retiring as governor, Stanley returned to Wichita and resumed his law practice.

Stanley died on Oct. 13, 1910. The Wichita Eagle reported:

"There was no other man about like him, just like him, or nearly like him at the bar or engaged in public life. His individuality was original. His personality more his own than men usually have. It was always intensely human, active and attractive."

F.W. "Woody" Hockaday

Tire dealer went the extra mile to make his maps

In 1915, F.W. "Woody" Hockaday put Wichita, Kansas City, Washington, D.C., and San Francisco on the map. And connected them by miles and miles of highways.

A pioneer mapmaker, Hockaday hired a road crew to mark 60,000 miles of highways across the nation. Then he handed out free Hockaday Road Maps at his tire store at Topeka and William.

"He was an inspiration for early mapmaking in Kansas and Sedgwick County," Ellington said. "He was another prime example of entrepreneurship in Wichita."

The Hockaday maps gained national recognition and were the forerunner of today's road map. Some of the highways that he helped mark are still well-traveled, including U.S. 54, K-96 and U.S. 81.

Originally from Caldwell, Hockaday came to Wichita in 1903 and worked for his uncle's hardware company. He soon had his own bicycle and motorcycle dealership, and eventually began selling automobile tires and batteries.

By 1915, he was marking the nation's highways.

The Wichita Eagle reported that "Hockaday Roads are finding a permanent place in the vocabulary of motorists in and near Wichita.

"With the intersection of Douglas and Lawrence avenues as the hub, Mr. Hockaday will radiate his roads in every direction. They will be designated from just ordinary roads by signs at every corner where a turn in the road is to be made."

F.W. "Woody" Hockaday also used unorthodox means to crusade for world peace.

Dave Williams/The Wichita Eagle

A parking lot is at the site of the store at William and Topeka.

The Hockaday road sign was a huge H with an arrow and the number of miles to the nearest city.

In 1915, Hockaday also initiated a service for drivers who had flat tires. Using a precursor of the tow truck, Hockaday had a fleet of cars to answer calls within a 10-mile radius of Wichita. The service was free.

"The only exertion necessary will be a walk to the nearest telephone to call one of the Hockaday free service cars," a 1915 Eagle advertisement said.

"Motorists can now drive with pleasure and without worrying about what they shall do if they have one of those awful blowouts. All they have to do is call Market 102. The cars are equipped with tanks of compressed air and a competent man will be on each car."

As Hockaday began promoting better highways through the distribution of his maps, he also turned to politics. A proponent of world peace, he was friends with presi-

dents Woodrow Wilson and Calvin Coolidge. The Hockadays attended Coolidge's inauguration.

But his political antics sometimes raised eyebrows.

When Franklin Roosevelt was giving a speech in Oklahoma in 1936, Hockaday jumped on stage and shined the president's shoes. It was his way of attracting attention to what he had to say about world peace. And in 1935, he dressed in red shorts and an Indian war bonnet, smeared his body with red paint and invaded the office of the assistant secretary of war, tossing feathers about the room and shouting, "Feathers instead of bullets."

"He wanted to be recognized for world peace," Ellington said. "You will have to admit rushing up on stage and shining Roosevelt's shoes is a little wild, a bit strange. In the balance of the thing, he did receive recognition from this strange event."

Hockaday also sponsored a campaign that said, "Kansas Grows the Best Wheat in the World." That campaign took him to all sections of the United States, where he distributed tiny sacks of Kansas wheat and helped the state gain the reputation as the "Breadbasket of the World."

He died in 1947, and the Hockaday Tire Store was razed two years later.

Col. Sam Amidon

Criminal attorney argued city's important cases

Col. Sam Amidon told people that when it came time for him to die, he had only one request:

"I want to die in the harness," he said. "I've been fighting all my life, and I couldn't bear the inactivity of a long illness. I'm not afraid of death, but I want it to come quickly, when it does come."

He got his wish. At the time of his death in 1925, Amidon was a national Democratic leader and one of the state's best criminal attorneys.

Between 1890 and his death, Amidon attended every Democratic national convention as a delegate. In 1917, he was elected to the national committee and later became vice chairman of the party.

Amidon was a friend of Woodrow Wilson, who as president offered Amidon the position of assistant attorney general of the United States.

Amidon turned the job down.

He was a man who seemed to generate power, but didn't abuse it. He was a lawyer always involved in

the most important cases in Wichita.

Born May 3, 1863, in Plainesville, Ohio, Amidon came to Wichita in 1886 and opened a law office.

Early on, he established a reputation as a fair and just lawyer, and he won the first case he handled.

In 1896, he became Sedgwick County's prosecuting attorney.

Upon his death, the Wichita Bar Association paid tribute to Amidon:

"As a practitioner before courts and juries, his work was characterized by exhaustive investigation of

"I envy the old pioneers, the old builders of the West, who died with their boots on."—Sam Amidon

the law involved, knowledge of the evidence and by a masterful presentation of the law and evidence and by his eloquent arguments."

Amidon was also known for his humanitarian interests. For 22 years, he was host of a Christmas dinner for Wichita's poor.

He was on the board of directors for several area banks and businesses, including First National Bank in Mount Hope, Kechi State Bank and Wichita Casket Co.

While he was a member of the Knights of Pythias, the title of colonel was bestowed on Amidon. It stuck.

On May 8, 1925, he suffered a heart attack. He was at his law office in the Fourth National Bank building and had just made reservations for a vacation on an ocean liner.

Local newspapers said he had felt ill but had continued his work and handled cases in the district court.

Amidon was sitting at his desk as the heart attack came on. He called his doctor at 6:20 p.m. Ten minutes later he was dead.

He had told his friends that that was the type of death he wanted.

"I envy the old pioneers, the old builders of the West, who died with their boots on," he once told a reporter. "That's the way I want to go, when my time comes—die in my office, in harness."

A street and a bridge in west Wichita are named for Amidon. His home at 1005 N. Market is now the law office of Crockett, Keeley & Gilhousen.

"Amidon was a powerhouse but he didn't play it up as a human being," Ellington said. "He generated power by the first-rate cases he accepted. He was a competent attorney and was always looked up to by the Wichita Bar Association."

J.J. Jones

Auto manufacturing company was a casualty of war

Wichita could have been known as another Detroit had it not been for World War I.

The Jones Motor Car Co., owned and operated by J.J. Jones, started manufacturing cars in Wichita in the fall of 1914.

The company, first at 122 W. Douglas and later at 801 E. 37th N., produced more than 3,000 vehicles before it closed in 1921. Most famous were the Jones Six cars, known for their bright colors, several coats of lacquer, soundness and ability to go 60 mph.

His automobile certainly wasn't a failure. It was a quality-item automobile.

Jones manufactured four car and two truck models. The Jones car designs were among the first to be streamlined and perhaps the first with a convex rear. His trucks were known for durability. They were especially made for oil field work and for heavy-duty transportation, and they had hard rubber tires.

Jones moved to Wichita in 1894 when he was 23. He operated several businesses in the downtown area, one of which manufactured the Jones Shaker Churn, a butter churn.

By February 1902, Jones owned a furniture store on West Douglas.

He later expanded the building and business to include a Ford motorcar and used car agency. At that time, automobile owners on the East Coast began to trade used cars for new cars on a large scale. Jones took advantage of this by traveling through the nation buying used

The Jones Motor Car Co. and its assembly line produced more than 3,000 vehicles between 1914 and 1921. One was the seven-passenger touring model.

J.J. Jones owned a furniture store and car dealership before starting his car company.

J.J. Jones' company manufactured four car and two truck models. The Jones car designs were among the first to be streamlined and perhaps the first with a convex rear.

cars and shipping them back to Wichita.

Jones eventually phased out the furniture, Ford and used car businesses and started the Jones Motor Co., said John Cyphert, former exhibit preparer at the Wichita-Sedgwick County Historical Museum.

On Nov. 1, 1914, he ran a full-page advertisement in The Wichita Daily Eagle promoting his six-cylinder "standardized car," which sold for $1,150 and was considered a moderately priced midsize car.

Jones moved his plant in 1915 to the Burton Stock Car complex on 37th North, the site of a large railroad stock car manufacturing company during the 1880s boom of Wichita. The complex, built in 1887, was nominated in 1988 to be placed on the National Register of Historic Places for its historical association with a number of industries in Wichita. In 1988, it was placed on the Register of Historic Kansas Places.

Today, the Coleman Co. maintains a plant in the complex.

Between 1915 and 1921, Jones built extensively, winding up with five buildings. The first, a mill building, contained a power plant, a machine shop and woodworking departments where the framework for passenger cars and trucks was built. Others housed the sheet metal work where vehicle bodies were covered and hoods were built; the upholstering, paint and enameling departments; the final assembly building where all the parts were brought together and the vehicles were completed; and a service building from which parts were shipped.

A fire Feb. 19, 1920, destroyed two buildings. Fourteen finished Jones Six automobiles and 100 car frames were lost in the blaze. Since 75 percent of the loss was covered by insurance, Jones quickly went back into production. His most expensive model was introduced the following year, a 1921 town car with a Victoria top and wire wheels. It cost $2,850.

Ellington said the aftermath of World War I and its effects on the economy destroyed the Jones auto company. Prices soared on even the smallest parts, and by 1921, Detroit had become a giant competitor. Jones closed the plant that same year. Today, the only Jones Six automobile in Wichita is on display in the Wichita-Sedgwick County Historical Museum, 204 S. Main.

Jones died in Wichita on Oct. 21, 1944.

"He held his own as a motorcar manufacturer. He possibly could have risen to unknown heights," Ellington said.

White Castle Burgers

50 cents' worth of meat started a chain reaction

In the annals of national history, Wichita will always be remembered for sporting the first hamburger stand.

Walt Anderson opened his five-stool stand in 1916 on East Douglas, near where The Wichita Eagle building stands today. After he borrowed $60 to buy equipment and supplies, newspaper accounts say, he didn't have enough money to buy ground beef.

On the morning of his opening day, he rushed to the W.A. Dye store and ordered 5 pounds of ground meat. As soon as it was wrapped, he grabbed the beef and promised to pay by noon. At noon, he returned to the store and paid his 50-cent bill in nickels, then bought another 50 cents' worth of meat.

"The credit of who invented the first hamburger should go to Walt Anderson," Ellington said. "He was the one who had the concept of pressing meat into a patty, puncturing holes to let the aroma come on through, and placing it on the grill. He'd place his onions and pickles on top of the patty and bun to absorb the juice of the hamburger. Before this, a hamburger was a ball in between two slices of bread."

So successful was the venture that within two years, Anderson opened another stand. By 1920, he owned four hamburger stands in Wichita and joined forces with Edgar Waldo "Billy" Ingram, a popular Wichita insurance and real estate man, to mass-produce hamburgers at 110 W. First.

The men agreed to call their hamburger stands White Castle. "White" signified purity and cleanliness, and "castle" represented strength, permanence and stability. Their buildings' architectural style was patterned after an old water tower in Chicago.

Because White Castle burgers were so cheap—a nickel apiece—they were almost always sold by the sack, to carry out. Within time, they were affectionately and not so affectionately nicknamed "gut

Edgar Waldo "Billy" Ingram was an insurance and real estate man before selling hamburgers.

Walt Anderson had to get his opening-day ground meat on credit; he paid the bill at noon.

bombs," "Whiteys," "sliders," "roachburgers," "Castles," "Whitey one-bites," and "belly busters."

During the Depression years The Eagle advertised White Castle burgers at six hamburgers for 25 cents.

Anderson was born in St. Mary's, Kan., on Nov. 26, 1880. He attended Baker University in Baldwin and came to Wichita around 1900. He did various odd jobs before getting into the restaurant and food-preparation business.

In 1916 he bought an old streetcar, did some remodeling and called it the Green Lunch Car. That was when he began experimenting with the hamburger.

At first, few people thought it was a worthy goal. The Eagle reported on Dec. 9, 1925:

"Hamburgers, the popular appetite satisfiers of the great Middle West, have never won world or nation-wide recognition, not even to the extent of securing a definition in the newest Webster's International dictionary. . . . Wichita has always been the capital of the ham-

burger country."

Now, of course, there are hamburger stands all over the nation. But then, Anderson had a theory about why the Midwest consumed more hamburgers than did other parts of the nation:

"The residents of the great Middle West have a diet composed of bread in one of its many forms, meat and vegetables," he said. "In that territory adjacent to the seaboard the sandwich will never become as popular as fish as a principal item of diet. However, in wheat, meat and vegetable country the hamburger can never be displaced."

Anderson, who lived at 455 S. Hillside, continued as head of the White Castle chain until 1933, when the headquarters was moved to Columbus, Ohio. He retired then.

He was an early supporter of Wichita aviation and had a pilot's license. His plane had the White Castle logo on it. He was also a Mason and worked in the Albert Pike Lodge. He died on Dec. 13, 1963.

When Anderson retired, Ingram became president of the White Castle system. He was born Dec. 28, 1880, in Leadville, Colo., in a slab house composed of two rooms and roofed with tin cans.

Walt Anderson and Billy Ingram opened the first White Castle stand at 110 W. First. Its architectural style was patterned after an old water tower in Chicago.

His family moved to Nebraska when he was 2. He came to Wichita in 1908 and was a partner in the insurance business with A.W. Hiner. Eventually, other partners came on board and the firm's name was changed to Lester, Ingram and Fox.

In 1912, Ingram's company was dissolved and he became a state agent for the farm and hail department of the Springfield Farm and Marine Insurance Co. By 1920, Ingram and Anderson had become close friends. Ingram decided to go into the hamburger business as a sideline. After 1921, he devoted his interest full time to the hamburger chain.

While in Wichita, Ingram was active in the Rotary Club, Masons and Wichita Community Chest. He also served as chairman of the Public Health Committee. He was an avid fly fisherman and hunter.

He died May 20, 1966, in Columbus, Ohio.

The Kings-X hamburger chain as Wichita residents know it today evolved from the departure of White Castle. Jimmy King was the regional manager for White Castle, and there was a gentleman's agreement that Kings-X would not penetrate the Wichita market for many years.

Today there are no White Castle stands in Wichita; the last one closed in 1938. The only four in Kansas are in Johnson County.

Artists,
Actors and
Opera Stars

"It has been such a long time since I heard from you or anyone in the States it worries me. How is Daddy? Tell him not to worry about me, especially as long as the USA keeps out of the war."
—Opera star Kathleen Kersting in a letter she wrote to family members in 1939.

John Noble

His seascapes grew from the prairie

The truth of the matter was that John Noble loved the prairie.

He loved its vastness and rolling landscapes. That's why he painted pictures of the ocean.

"There's not much difference between the prairie and the ocean—that is, the prairie I used to know," Noble once told a reporter. "I began to feel that the vastness, the bulk, the overwhelming power of the prairie is the same in its immensity as the sea, only the sea is changeless, and the plains, as I knew, were passing."

Born in Wichita on March 15, 1874, Noble was one of the first Kansas artists to achieve international fame.

He generated interest by his unique style of painting, which was both realistic and impressionistic. He characteristically used lots of rich colors and deep tones to create paintings of dramatic seascapes.

His parents, Elizabeth and John Noble Sr., arrived in Wichita in 1872. Their home was at 1029 N. Market. Newspaper clippings report that the young Noble began drawing horses and cattle when he was 5 years old. Those drawings attracted the attention of Victor Murdock, then a writer for The Wichita Eagle.

As Murdock wrote, Noble painted and illustrated stories about

John Noble painted "Cleopatra at the Bath," which hung at the Carey Hotel and at which Carry A. Nation threw a rock.

Wild Bill Hickok, Bob Dalton and other characters from the Old West. His childhood idol was William Mathewson, the original Buffalo Bill. He despised school and quit after eighth grade but continued to read works by Homer, Shakespeare, Blake and Milton.

One of his earliest artworks was a life-size pastel titled "Cleopatra at the Bath." It was a painting of a nude that hung in the Carey Hotel. On Dec. 27, 1900, the painting was

slightly damaged when Carry A. Nation threw a rock at it in an effort to clean up the corruption of Wichita.

The painting was hung on the wall opposite the bar mirror so patrons who stepped up to the bar could gaze into the mirror and see Cleopatra at the same time.

Nation not only smashed the looking glass but the painting as well. Only the painting's glass covering was damaged, however.

After the turn of the century, Noble left Wichita and studied at the Cincinnati Academy of Fine Arts and later in Paris, London and Brussels, Belgium. While in Europe, he painted and worked as a seaman along the coast of France.

Noble impressed the art crowds in Europe and New York with his stories about the Old West, particularly stories about Buffalo Bill. He traditionally wore a wrinkled old suit and Windsor tie and a wide-brimmed brown Texas hat.

He studied at some of the best art schools and was accepted in the best art circles. Nevertheless, his idol was Buffalo Bill, and he told people he wanted to be buried beside him.

Noble died on Jan. 6, 1934, from an overdose of paraldehyde—a drug used then for the treatment of alcohol. He is buried in Highland Cemetery near Mathewson.

Sidney Toler

"Charlie Chan" got his start on his father's stage

With his heavily lidded eyes, high cheekbones and Confucius-style delivery, Sidney Toler made a name for himself in the movies.

He played Charlie Chan, the famous fictional sleuth who dazzled movie audiences in the 1930s with

such bits of wisdom as: "Never tamper with gold fillings in a gift horse's teeth."

Toler was the son of Hooper G. and Sallie Toler, a prominent family who lived at the corner of Second and Wichita.

When the family moved to Wich-

ita in 1878, Hooper Toler opened a grocery store. In 1882, he went into the real estate business, and five years later he bought a stock farm with a racetrack that he named Tolerville. The family's stable of racing horses included John R. Gentry, called the second fastest

Sidney Toler landed the role of famous sleuth Charlie Chan in 1938.

stallion in the world at that time.

But in 1889, when Wichita's economy burst, the Tolers lost much of their money, Ellington said. They had to sell their racing horses and the farm.

In 1900, Hooper Toler bought a large entertainment house on the southwest corner of St. Francis and First. He renamed it Toler Auditorium. The building was octagonal with wings on the side. The exits were 54 feet wide, or nearly the width of a city street, and designed to accommodate a flow of people. The auditorium was razed in 1917.

Many famous artists performed on the stage of the auditorium, including Sarah Bernhardt and John Mansfield.

It was in that auditorium that Sidney Toler started his career as an actor. His mother wrote plays and encouraged her son to become a theater professional.

The Wichita Eagle reported on Jan. 29, 1939, in an article about Toler that his first theatrical experience was in a play, "Tom Sawyer."

"Mrs. Toler treasures a letter Mark Twain wrote her at the time in which he stated he was surprised to learn 'Tom Sawyer' could be made into a play. It was the first time it ever was so presented."

When he was 18, Sidney Toler left Wichita to attend the University of Kansas. Upon graduation, he performed in Kansas City's Ninth Street theaters and toured for several years with Julia Marlow. He appeared as a character actor in movies such as "The Trumpet Blows," "Madam X," "The Gorgeous Hussy," "Gold Is Where You Find It" and "The Kid From Kokomo." Other movies included "Blond Venus" featuring Marlene Dietrich, "The Way to Love," "Upper World," "Massacre," "Registered Nurse" and "Up the River."

In 1938, he landed the role of Charlie Chan—even though he was 6 feet tall and had blue eyes.

"It's fascinating to me that a man raised on the plains of Kansas turned out to be one of the greatest Chinese impersonators of all time," Ellington said. "He carried his role with dignity and certainly was loved by the folks back home. People were proud of their native son."

Throughout his career, Toler remained fond of Wichita and sometimes wrote letters to friends back home. One of them appeared in The Eagle in 1939:

"From time to time I have felt a great nostalgia for my hometown, but have not come back because I know that the Wichita I knew no longer exists. I would like to see some of my old friends there, though, and will before so very long. I hope."

Toler died in February 1941. He was 59 years old.

Toler Auditorium had exits 54 feet wide, nearly the width of a city street. The building on the southwest corner of St. Francis and First was razed in 1917.

C.A. Seward

Prairie printmaker won national acclaim

Coy Avon Seward was one of those central Kansas farm boys who never lost his love for the state and its people. His name, though, was a different matter.

"He hated that name, he always went by C.A. Seward," said Betty Dickerson, a longtime friend of Seward's.

And it was as C.A. Seward that he won international acclaim as an art-

C.A. Seward works in his studio in the Butts Building circa 1910.

ist. A charter member of the Wichita Art Association, Seward helped found a regional print society in the 1920s known as the Prairie Printmakers. The group grew in prestige as its members won national awards.

"He was not always in the foreground of things, but he was always one of the organizers of groups," said Dave Thompson, Seward's grandson who now lives in Wilmington, Del.

Born March 4, 1884, near Chase, Seward graduated from Chase High School in 1901 and began working in the lumber business at nearby Ellinwood.

"His friends saw he had a knack for design, and he spent almost as much time designing letterheads, stationery and outside billboards as he did in the lumber business," Thompson said.

Seward soon left Ellinwood and studied at Washburn University in Topeka and Bethany College in Lindsborg. While at Bethany, he met Birger Sandzen (1871-1954), a Swedish immigrant who helped establish Lindsborg as an artists' colony.

In 1908, Seward married his childhood sweetheart, Mabel Eliza-

beth Drew, and moved to Wichita. For a number of years, he was manager of the local branch of Capper Engraving Co. He later became head of the art department of Western Lithograph Co.

His work as an lithographer won several awards and was exhibited in Santa Fe and Taos, N.M., Los Angeles, Chicago and Paris. In 1932, he wrote "Metal-Plate Lithography," a book describing a new process of lithography.

Although his reputation grew worldwide, Seward remained rooted in Kansas.

"If he would have moved anywhere, it would have been back to the farm at Chase, where he grew up. He was a Kansan," Thompson said.

From his offices in the Butts Building and at Western Lithograph Co., Seward designed Kansas Day celebration postcards and Dye Chili factory advertisements. The Butts Building was on the southwest corner of First and Broadway; Western Lithograph Co. was at the southwest corner of First and Topeka.

He also, through the Prairie

Printmakers, supported other artists struggling to make a name.

"At that time, Wichita was famous for its art," said Dickerson, a former instructor of painting at the Wichita Center for the Arts. Dickerson's husband, the late William J. Dickerson, was a Wichita printmaker and director of the Wichita Art Association school.

"There were seven print companies in Wichita. And people wanting graphic illustrations from across the nation would come here for the artwork," she said. "This attracted artists and the need for the Prairie Printmakers group."

Local historians note that Seward's painting of early Wichita is considered one of the most accurate renditions of the town's genesis. Although no photographs existed of early-day Wichita, Seward meticulously interviewed old settlers and asked them to describe the town.

Seward showed a lifelong devotion to art education, promotion and organization. He died in 1939 from a strep infection. He was 54.

This thoroughly researched painting of early Wichita is considered by local historians to be one of the most accurate renditions of the town's genesis.

Kathleen Kersting

City's opera star led a fairy-tale life

Kathleen Kersting's fairy-tale life was the pride of Wichita.

From her early childhood, Kersting sang and impressed neighbors, family and members of the South Lawrence Christian Church with her dramatic and musical abilities. When she was 13 years old, she gave her first public concert, at the Wichita Theater. That year, in 1922, French vocalist Madam Emma Calve visited Wichita and heard Kersting sing.

Calve demanded of Kersting's parents that Kathleen be permitted to study with her in New York.

"It was something for a Kansas youngster to have such a contrast in lifestyles," Ellington said.

Born in Enid, Okla., in 1908, Kersting came to Wichita as a child with her parents, who opened the Kersting Hotel at 320 N. Market.

After she went to study in New York, her parents invested all they could to support their daughter. Two years later, Kersting returned to Wichita for a concert to raise money for further study. Her parents' resources were exhausted, so the Wichita Rotary Club agreed to help. The local Rotarians raised $15,000 for Kersting to study three more years, this time in France and Italy.

In 1928, Kersting made her operatic debut in Saluzzo, Italy, playing Marguerite in "Faust." Newspaper critics described her as "the girl with the golden nightingale in her throat," and said, "She sang with grace, with ease, with soul."

Two years later Kersting was an international opera star, giving sold-out concert tours in both Europe and the United States.

During the 1930s, she worked with the Chicago Civic Opera Company and toured Europe. When World War II broke out, Kersting's fairy-tale life began to tarnish. She had married a German officer, who was stationed in Germany, and was unable to leave or communicate with family and friends. For several months in the summer and fall of 1939, no one heard from her. Then she found a friend in Milan, Italy, who was able to mail a letter to Wichita family members.

The letter was published in The Wichita Eagle:

"It has been such a long time since I heard from you or anyone in the States it worries me," Kersting wrote. "How is Daddy? Tell him not to worry about me, especially as long as the USA keeps out of the war."

Toward the end of the war, Kersting was forced to abandon her singing career and worked in a German munitions factory.

"She was having a hard life," Ellington said. "When the war subsided, things got better for her. She divorced her husband and went

Kathleen Kersting gave her first public concert in Wichita when she was 13. She went on to become an opera star who drew crowds in Europe as well as the United States.

back to her first love." That love was singing.

After the war, Kersting worked with the U.S. government in cultural exchange programs, especially in Germany. Her last concert in Wichita was in 1952. She then returned to Europe to teach.

The highlight of her singing career came in 1947, when President Truman asked her to sing for him at the White House.